Bible Interpretations

Twenty-first Series
July 5 – September 27, 1896

II Samuel, I Chronicles, Proverbs

Bible Interpretations

Twenty-first Series

II Samuel, I Chronicles, Proverbs

These Bible Interpretations were published in the Inter-Ocean Newspaper in Chicago, Illinois during the late eighteen nineties.

By
Emma Curtis Hopkins

President of the Emma Curtis Hopkins Theological Seminary at Chicago, Illinois

Bible Interpretations: Twenty-first Series

By Emma Curtis Hopkins

© WiseWoman Press 2014

Managing Editor: Michael Terranova

ISBN: 978-0945385-72-1

WiseWoman Press

Vancouver, WA 98665

www.wisewomanpress.com

www.emmacurtishopkins.com

CONTENTS

	Foreword by Rev. Natalie R. Jean ix
	Introduction by Rev. Michael Terranova xi
I.	The Lord Reigneth 1
	II Samuel 2:1-11
II.	Adeptship 11
	II Samuel 5:1-12
III.	The Ark 21
	II Samuel 6:1-12
IV.	Purpose Of An Adept 31
	II Samuel 7:4-16
	The Inter Ocean Newspaper, July 26, 1896
V.	Individual Emancipation 43
	II Samuel 9:1-13
VI.	The Almighty Friend 53
	II Samuel 10:8-19
VII.	Missing 63
VIII.	Individual Emancipation 65
	II Samuel 15:1-12
IX.	Absalom's Defeat And Death 77
	II Samuel 18:9-17
X.	The Crown Of Effort 87
	I Chronicles 22:6-16
XI.	"Thy Gentleness Hath Made Me Great" 97
	II Samuel 22
XII.	A Fool For Christ's Sake 109
	Proverbs 16:7-33
XIII.	The Lord Is A Strong Tower 117
	Proverbs 28:10
	List of Bible Interpretation Series 132

Editors Note

All lessons starting with the Seventh Series of Bible Interpretations will be Sunday postings from the Inter-Ocean Newspaper in Chicago, Illinois. Many of the lessons in the following series were retrieved from the International New Thought Association Archives, in Mesa, Arizona by, Rev Joanna Rogers. Many others were retrieved from libraries in Chicago, and the Library of Congress, by Rev. Natalie Jean.

All the lessons follow the Sunday School Lesson Plan published in "Peloubet's International Sunday School Lessons". The passages to be studied are selected by an International Committee of traditional Bible Scholars.

Some of the Emma's lessons don't have a title. In these cases the heading will say "Comments and Explanations of the Golden Text," followed by the Bible passages to be studied.

Foreword

By Rev. Natalie R. Jean

I have read many teachings by Emma Curtis Hopkins, but the teachings that touch the very essence of my soul are her Bible Interpretations. There are many books written on the teachings of the Bible, but none can touch the surface of the true messages more than these Bible interpretations. With each word you can feel and see how Spirit spoke through Emma. The mystical interpretations take you on a wonderful journey to Self Realization.

Each passage opens your consciousness to a new awareness of the realities of life. The illusions of life seem to disappear through each interpretation. Emma teaches that we are the key that unlocks the doorway to the light that shines within. She incorporates ideals of other religions into her teachings, in order to understand the commonalities, so that there is a complete understanding of our Oneness. Emma opens our eyes and mind to a better today and exciting future.

Emma Curtis Hopkins, one of the Founders of New Thought teaches us to love ourselves, to speak our Truth, and to focus on our Good. My life has moved in wonderful directions because of her teachings. I know the only thing that can move me in this world is God. May these interpretations guide you to a similar path and may you truly remember that "There Is Good For You and You Ought to Have It."

Introduction

Emma Curtis Hopkins was born in 1849 in Killingsly, Connecticut. She passed on April 8, 1925. Mrs. Hopkins had a marvelous education and could read many of the worlds classical texts in their original language. During her extensive studies she was always able to discover the Universal Truths in each of the world's sacred traditions. She quotes from many of these teachings in her writings. As she was a very private person, we know little about her personal life. What we do know has been gleaned from other people or from the archived writings we have been able to discover.

Emma Curtis Hopkins was one of the greatest influences on the New Thought movement in the United States. She taught over 50,000 people the Universal Truth of knowing "God is All there is." She taught many of founders of early New Thought, and in turn these individuals expanded the influence of her teachings. All of her writings encourage the student to enter into a personal relationship with God. She presses us to deny anything except the Truth of this spiritual Presence in every area of our lives. This is the central focus of all her teachings.

The first six series of Bible Interpretations were presented at her seminary in Chicago, Illinois. The remaining Series', probably close to thirty, were printed in the Inter Ocean Newspaper in Chicago. Many of the lessons are no longer available for various reasons. It is the intention of WiseWoman Press to publish as many of these Bible Interpretations as possible. Our hope is that any missing lessons will be found or directed to us.

I am very honored to join the long line of people that have been involved in publishing Emma Curtis Hopkins's Bible Interpretations. Some confusion exists as to the numbering sequence of the lessons. In the early 1920's many of the lessons were published by the Highwatch Fellowship. Inadvertently the first two lessons were omitted from the numbering system. Rev. Joanna Rogers has corrected this mistake by finding the first two lessons and restoring them to their rightful place in the order. Rev. Rogers has been able to find many of the missing lessons at the International New Thought Alliance archives in Mesa, Arizona. Rev. Rogers painstakingly scoured the archives for the missing lessons as well as for Mrs. Hopkins other works. She has published much of what was discovered. WiseWoman Press is now publishing the correctly numbered series of the Bible Interpretations.

In the early 1940's, there was a resurgence of interest in Emma's works. At that time, Highwatch Fellowship began to publish many of her writings, and it was then that *High Mysticism*, her seminal work was published. Previously, the material contained in High Mysticism was only available as individual lessons and was brought together in book form for the first time. Although there were many errors in these first publications and many Bible verses were incorrectly quoted, I am happy to announce that WiseWoman Press is now publishing *High Mysticism* in the a corrected format. This corrected form was scanned faithfully from the original, individual lessons.

The next person to publish some of the Bible Lessons was Rev. Marge Flotron from the Ministry of Truth International in Chicago, Illinois. She published the Bible Lessons as well as many of Emma's other works. By her initiative, Emma's writings were brought to a larger audience when DeVorss & Company, a longtime publisher of Truth Teachings, took on the publication of her key works.

In addition, Dr. Carmelita Trowbridge, founding minister of The Sanctuary of Truth in Alhambra, California, inspired her assistant minister, Rev. Shirley Lawrence, to publish many of Emma's works, including the first three series of Bible Interpretations. Rev. Lawrence created mail order courses for many of these Series. She has graciously passed on any information she had, in order to assure that these works continue to inspire individuals and groups who are called to further study of the teachings of Mrs. Hopkins.

Finally, a very special acknowledgement goes to Rev Natalie Jean, who has worked diligently to retrieve several of Emma's lessons from the Library of Congress, as well as libraries in Chicago. Rev. Jean hand-typed many of the lessons she found on microfilm. Much of what she found is on her website, www.highwatch.net.

It is with a grateful heart that I am able to pass on these wonderful teachings. I have been studying dear Emma's works for fifteen years. I was introduced to her writings by my mentor and teacher, Rev. Marcia Sutton. I have been overjoyed with the results of delving deeply into these Truth Teachings.

In 2004, I wrote a Sacred Covenant entitled "Resurrecting Emma," and created a website, www.emmacurtishopkins.com. The result of creating this covenant and website has brought many of Emma's works into my hands and has deepened my faith in God. As a result of my love for these works, I was led to become a member of Wise-Woman Press and to publish these wonderful teachings. God is Good.

My understanding of Truth from these divinely inspired teachings keeps bringing great Joy, Freedom, and Peace to my life.

Dear reader; It is with an open heart that I offer these works to you, and I know they will touch you as they have touched me. Together we are living in the Truth that God is truly present, and living for and through each of us.

The greatest Truth Emma presented to us is "My Good is my God, Omnipresent, Omnipotent and Omniscient."

Rev. Michael Terranova
WiseWoman Press
Vancouver, Washington, 2010

LESSON I

The Lord Reigneth

II Samuel 2:1-11

"Still, through our paltry stir and strife,
Glows down the wished deal."
Lowell

The golden text of this lesson is "The Lord reigneth."

The inference we catch from it is that we all and each have some idea that is forever coloring our affairs and shaping our course in life whether we believe it or not.

The bread to get out of the lesson is that the divine flavor in our daily life is indestructible. The direction to hear from its words is that we may still keep on doing the generous, the noble, the magnanimous things we first started out to do; this time not with thinking them a part of the actual substance, but knowing that they are the instinctive pushings of the conquering ideal.

This lesson teaches that people need not think they have done anything if they have given great things in charity, done great kindness in mercy, lent their goods in benevolence, for it was not what they did that counted, but what they were intrinsically. Yet the intrinsic good in one always does the magnanimous thing.

This lesson takes up David at one period of his life and makes him exhibit the fact that whatever ideal has its swing going in our life causes us to move our feet and shape our conduct to finally exhibit this ideal plainly. Nothing can stop it. We may be exiles, failures, despised, and rejected, but that divinity line is at its invariable business of exposing itself if our ideal is divine.

David had been seven and one-half years exiled from the court of King Saul, but out he came and took his own kingship in good season. He had tried every way to help Saul keep the kingdom, but the divinity line ran David's way, and Saul had to move out of the path.

Saul stands for the world's dealings with us. If we take Abner's place we try to give the world it's wished for supremacy. Finally it falls in spite of our effort, as verse 10 of this chapter says. If we take David's place we do not try to give anything a great value which insists upon perishing. We keep our eye on the imperishable.

David had served Saul, supposing he was King. We serve the world supposing its cries are imperative. David found Saul a poor guide. We find that it is our privilege to sit in authority over the world with a newly vested power, when we see that its cries are its weakness, not its authority.

The story of David is ever the story of every human being who keeps his eye on divine things and builds his life around them. David was knocked about and hidden out of sight, misrepresented and hunted, but he was always greater and nobler than his misfortunes. His eye was on the great, therefore he was great. His eye was on the invincible, therefore he was invincible.

He tells in an object lesson just how we can come out, here on this planet, if we never think that we must do in Rome as the Romans do, or act in the world as the worldly act.

David never imitated Saul. He was not puffed up with a fictitious value by Samuel's anointing as poor Saul had been ready to topple over and be nobody if Samuel withdrew his power. He stood on his own feet.

The Example of King Saul

The example of Saul made something by Samuel's favor, and made nothing by his disfavor, is a plain lesson of how dependent some people become upon the praises of their fellow men. There is a living example now in the world to illustrate this same tendency of the human mind. It is the little Dalai Llama of Tibet, of the Indian faith. His own qualities are whipped aside, and he is imbued with the notions of certain adepts. Then he speaks and moves and thinks exactly like them.

This lesson of David today, II, Samuel 2:1-11, gives us as nations a clear lesson; also as individuals a plain talk about where we stand and how we are coming out. It enunciates the startling prophecy that we are going to stop the use of gold and silver on this earth. We are going to see money demonetized, dethroned. There is a great ideal in all men's minds of a kingdom where they do not settle matters by metals, but by souls. That ideal has now been openly preached. It is very dangerous to fictitious values when actual values are exposed. Today's lesson is so vitally instructive that it seems a pity that somebody other than a simple interpreter should present it to the people. But as it is left to the unprejudiced interpreter it must go as it is meant.

In spite of Abner we notice that Saul's reign failed. Samuel had said Saul was great, and Abner worked to keep up the delusion, but uselessly. His reign ceased.

Now, the key of David was his touch of the conquering soul. It made his eyes victorious over opposition wherever they looked. It made his hands master whatever they touched. It made his mind a smelting heat, upon whatever he thought, so that nothing that opposed him could prosper. This committee did not touch the soul; they only longed for the soul. They did not have even the ability of an Indian fakir in the business of stopping in the fictitious values placed on metals, for they said they could not help clutching after high salaries. This showed that the same old adepts were running things and they were in their path.

This lesson says that inasmuch as we have not raised any pious pulpit orators with adeptship enough in them to shut off delusions, there is one with his touch of eye and hand on divinity who will shut off both the master and the pupil out on the land.

A New Dawn is Breaking

A new era is breaking. David is here. That is, some soul quality now becomes visible in life. The soulless banking, manufacturing, trading that have grown out of calling two valueless metals the touchstone of rights to breath and peace, shall suddenly of rights to breath and peace, shall suddenly cease, and a divine authority from the divinity spark in a whole world full of people shall arise up and act.

Some think this David era must be brought by war and famine. This lesson says no, very little of that.

Nobody dreams who wrote the books of Samuel, but whoever they were, they wrote out their highest ideal when they described David. They gave him two wives and many other so-called advantages on the material basis to show how the divinity line adjusts affairs so that men are prospered on both the mental and material planes.

They could not swing to an ideal so high as not to need any wives and concubines. The disciples of

Jesus swung as high as that. The disciples of David could not get out of sword-thrusting and stone-slinging to carry along their hero, but the historians of Jesus describe him as inoffensive as a lamb, yet as conquering as omnipotence.

All the poets have written that the highest ideals must get themselves demonstrated. Lately there have been no positive expressions as to how Czars and Queens and Presidents should act. The people have raised no adepts with dictatorial edicts. Instead of that our newspapers plainly state that we all wonder what these potentates will do. The potentates do not know anything on their own accounts, and so there is nothing done.

Nothing is defined that they must do, and, as they have no touch of their own soul, they have no ideals defined except that set up by the adepts, viz. Money. Riches. Let us get rich-rich-rich with money.

Just at this hour, therefore, the people are Saul's plight. That is, up and down, as money jumps.

The Soul Spark Within Us

Whoever can keep his head steady and stand to the soul spark within himself that has ability to put him into right places will see the world jumping. For the world does not like to jump. It likes to be judged and to judge, by the soul standards that does not fluctuate. Not even one or all Rothschilds combined could change the world's value; even the soul of the poorest wench that asks vainly for pennies at the roughest corners.

How ought a man to act who has begged for his only definitely stated goal? Exactly as men are now acting. How good and wise could a man be who had his ideal plainly set up as a power? What men with strength in, with strengthened passions, strength in knowledge of wisdom, speak, and write and move so as then what other men could do just as well as David did.

Is there a higher ideal defined and recognized than Jesus? There certainly was what was defined by him as coming to men out of greater works and wiser words than he was using. He told of coming again in a far more powerful touch of the soul and of coming as a visible power and with whose glory and authority none could withstand. Told of a touch of the soul with such energy enough in it to lift all men out of the toils of their neighbors. They should all cast off the clutches of their fellow men. They should all stand on their own independence.

He did not teach that each man is dependent on the other men. He taught that each is by divine origin independent of his neighbors.

The Soul Is Self-Living

He saw that as the divine soul is self-living, so every man is self living. "As the Father hath life in himself, so hath, he given the son to have life in himself?" There is nothing in that text that hints at my scrambling to get my dinner-pail filled with pork and beans by working for a corporation in a faithful manner. There is nothing in that text that hints at my sustaining my life by eating potatoes which I earned by spinning my thoughts over sick bodies and decrepit mind at $1 per spin.

The Samuel section tells that David got his thoughts kindled at the divine fire enough so that he had directions as to where to go next and what to do next on some lines. On other lines he was as deaf as other men. He had enough fire so that no poor opinions of him shot from a thousand adepts could change his self-estimate.

His gave us a good lesson by thus holding himself on his own base. He dipped his oars into the tideless water of inspiration, so that all men felt his majesty when he spoke to them or looked at them. Nothing that came sweeping over his life stopped that inspiration.

This section has its particular application. Take it to heart. It means that there is a miracle in the sky of your life which shall show its golden banners this week in some sweet fashion, but later on will be the daily occurrence in your life.

The new way which comes in on the Davidian Chariot stirs up our native independence of men, events and methods. It is not Christian to depend on men, events, or methods. It is Christian to be as miraculously cared for as the archangels.

The story of David urges to use that substance which can do with us as miraculously as with him.

The story of Jesus emphasizes it. The David *** over heart forever reminds us of it ****.

Never mind who says otherwise, that fictitious values of men and the world are left alone. Find that living thing of an unfailing worth. Its every word a miracle.

The story of David urges to **** that substance which can do with us miraculously as with him. The story of Jesus emphasizes it. The divine-laid soul over our heart forever reminds us of its love.

Never mind who says otherwise **** fictitious, values of men and the **** alone. Find that living thing ****, unfailing worth. Its every **** miracle.

The Chicago Inter Ocean Newspaper, July 5, 1896

**** Words missing on micro-fiche from newspaper archives.

LESSON II

Adeptship

II Samuel 5:1-12

"You know well it is not music, nor the gymnasium, nor the schools that mold young men; it is much more the public proclamations, the public examples. If you take one who has no high purpose, one who mocks at morals, and crown him in a the atrum every one who sees it imitates it. The character of a city is determined by the men it crowns." —Aeschines

"The true ruler seeks not to obtain all he can from the people, but to do all he can for the people" — Notes

ADEPTSHIP

The subject of this Bible lesson is called "Patriotism" by the international committee. Its real title is "Adeptship." As a lesson, it is quite dependent on last week's interpretation, for that gave the first principles of adeptship as related to nations.

The coming series of Sunday lessons for six months are to be devoted to national movements. The last six months have had sections relating wholly to individual life. But each man, woman, child, does keep pace with the general government, so all through the coming course each individual may trace his experience, in the main, for each week by reading of the kingdoms of Israel and Judah, united under David's reign, 1048 B.C.

The pith and point of last week's lesson showed how Isaiah's prophecy concerning silver and gold, with their images and superscriptions printed upon them, at the direction of men with the adept type of mind, is about being fulfilled, where he says: "Ye shall defile (or erase) the covering of the graven images of silver, and the molten images of gold. "Thou shalt cast them away. Thou shalt say, 'Get thee hence.'"

It taught nations the importance of raising adepts among children by pointing out to them the original state of mind belonging to them, telling them how to restore themselves to their own original state of mind, and assuring them of the supernal majestic authority vested in each and every one of them.

David attended to the name of the Lord of hosts as the "I am" of himself. Saul attended to Samuel's psychologic directions. "The people that do know their God shall be wise and do exploits," said Daniel's teacher; David exemplified it. He knew the name of his God. Saul just knew what Samuel told him, and nothing else.

There have been some Oriental adepts lately traveling through America with careful directions about sitting in negative attitudes of mind and body and repeating the name "Ohm." They have taught their scholars, or yogis, to sit and gaze down their spines; also to breathe the atmospheric air in by one nostril and out at the other for stated lengths of time by day and by night.

The Oriental Adepts

They have promised the sure finding of God the Omnipotent by these operations. And nobody has seemed to remember that the Oriental nations that have gazed at their spines for ages and ages, repeating the name "Ohm" till they have fallen to dust, have not seemed to be living proofs of the sure finding of God.

The lessons to be read from the coming Bible sections, started by last week's interpretation, are plain on the point of restoring ourselves to our own original state of mind by letting go of everything we have been taught and attending to what we know. For all that we have been taught has formulated a mask, has made up for us a fictitious mind, while what we know at our own headquarters is real substance.

The golden text of today's subject is: "David went on and grew great." The verses that tell about his sudden enlargement are to be found in II Samuel 5:1-12. The great hint in the section is, that the divine "I am" does not scramble and whirr to do mighty things, but yet mighty works are accomplished by the divine "I am." David's greatness was offered to him quietly, and he took it quietly, and nothing could interfere with him that opposed him.

This principle of power, through repose, is being talked and written about a great deal nowadays. One book tells us that if we go into a picture gallery and try to remember and study and judge of all the fine pictures, we are harassed and jaded, but if we sit quietly and let all the fine pictures come to us we go away remembering and knowing them all without weariness. One metaphysical healer has three hundred patients sometimes on her list. Somebody asked her if she went in thought to them all, and she answered: "No, I let them come to me." She has her mind's eye on the healing God, and they have their mind's eye on her. So they catch the healing streams through her sieve. The consequence, of course, is that they have her sieve marks. That is, their characteristics resemble hers.

The Bible lessons are tremendous in their enunciations concerning keeping our mind's eye on the divine God for ourselves and letting sieves alone, at the earliest possible moment. Jesus Christ did not have a sieve, and he refused to be a sieve. He resolved himself back into his original mind and that being the one only God, his name is the name by which David knew and conquered adversity. It is the name of the "I am," which has been positively promised to hasten man into his authoritative seat without dragging him through a lifetime of effort, or taking away his native substance.

Verse 1 says: "Then came all the tribes of Israel to David." By attending to his governing and all-knowing soul authority David became an adept. That one who can stamp gold and silver with values, or erase their values, at will. One who can change the minds and faces of nations to suit himself. One who has his own way about pretty much everything he deals with.

No Conflict of Rule

The masses have to have an adept of some sort to direct them till they are told of their own native powers and authority. Then they are adepts on their own account. And, though millions upon millions should become men in authority by the divine way of taking their own native throneship, there would be no conflict of rule, for at that throne place there is only one. "E plutibus unum."

In coming to David the men of antiquity came as near to themselves, to their own "I am", as they could get by the light of the instructions they had had respecting national affairs. Just so the men of modern days went to the present President of the United States and gave him authority over them as representing their highest ideal according to the light they had had respecting national affairs.

England praised these men very highly for having so glorious an ideal and proclaimed that by having such a noble man in the American chair of state the wheels and spindles of her countless mills had been set to whirring and financial prosperity had been set blazing in all Great Britain.

The world is prophesied to come as with one mighty impulse to Jesus Christ, eventually, as representing the highest ideal of all men as a national ruler. And the beauty of his reign is promised to be that each man of the world shall find his own self to be the vested authority when he offers Jesus Christ the authority. For in him is freedom from the domination of man over man.

The men of antiquity did much more wisely in looking to David as their highest ideal of rulership than some of our modern peoples have done, according to the way history reads for he actually shepherded and protected his people, instead of making them the prey of other nations as some of the modern heads of state have done with their confiding subjects.

But in looking to David those people all admitted they had heard of and believed in one to come with far more wonderful wisdom in the art of kingcraft than David could possibly exhibit. In looking to the modern magnates the people of today also admit the possibility of a higher ideal, but not the probability.

How this lesson says that when any people are feeling that the present ordering of affairs is intrenched so securely that no different or better order can possibly arrive, they may read verses six and nine of this fifth chapter of Samuel.

The city of Jebus represented for all time any magnate and his colleagues who should think that any state of affairs they had subscribed to and were maintaining was so strong that it could not be overthrown.

The Jebusites2 said that their position was so fortified that if only the lame and blind were left in charge of the posts no enemy could prevail against it.

There is one magnate with its devotees now so intrenched in confidence that nothing can dissolve or annul it, that whoever has his hand on a good box of it feels as secure as if his hand were on the divine "I am."

David Overwhelms Jebus

This magnate has no vital value in itself. Jebus, by standing for any magnate with devotees, stands also for the money power on this earth, as well as for Queen Victoria, with her confidence in the impregnability of her fortified realm, or the new Czar with his certainty that nothing dare interfere with him.

David, with his eye on the Divine Presence suddenly dissolved the fortress of Jebus and changed the name of the city from Jebus to Jerusalem. There was no substantial excellence, no vital value, in Jebus and the Jebusites. There was vital value, substantial excellence, in the City of the Eternal God, upon whom David's soul was set. Thus the Absolute was, in a sense, met face to face with the fictitious, when David said his soul hated the masquerading claims of Jebus. (Verse 8)

There is great spirit rising throughout the earth, in opposition to the placing of so much power in the silver and gold metals found in the ground and graven over with images and superscriptions telling of values they do not originally possess. This spirit is the David power, when it is plainly expressed and exposed to plain sight. There is no doubt about the intrenchments of nations and individuals in any of their positive positions being in near danger of dissolution when David gets in sight of them, however peaceably his army may be coming. That is, nothing today counted upon as powerful is going to withstand the soul's onslaught, no matter how weakly and softly its watchers may be marching on.

The money power in which the Jebusites of today are intrenched is about to fall. By some mysterious alchemy of the watchers of the eternal, it is to be suddenly dissolved. The present ideas of governments are to be suddenly erased from the mind of man. The present systems are to be suddenly met face to face with some practical proposition that shall supersede them as easily as David took Jebus and made it Zion.

This is by the divine endowment of some man or woman or army or nation with the adeptship of the "I Am" on the throne of their own being.

Ideal of Israelites

Nations have been told that the adepts of the Orient have been secretly running their machinery for generations. If so, how low the ideal — far lower than that of the Israelites of antiquity when they called David to the throne. People are beginning to discover that the multitudes have bowed their heads and said "yes" when strong minds and oratorical tongues have said so about as long as they can.

Jesus Christ was met by the strong edicts of adepts with power to print values and declare intrenchments. "What went ye out for to see? A reed shaken with the wind?" he asked them. He was no reed bowing "yes" to the low ideals of Orient, or Occident. He was a changeless rock of shelter, protection, of the world.

Over the fortified states of modern civilization the melting radiance of something like a new light is breaking. Around the trembling inhabitants of a world the protecting arms of a new dispensation are stretching. This Bible section says it is near.

The Oriental teachers say it is "Ohm." The metaphysicians say it is God. The Christian Bible says it is Jesus Christ, dissolver of kingdoms.

July 12, 1896

LESSON III

The Ark

II Samuel 6:1-12

The subject of this lesson is "The Ark." In ancient times the ark was the highest symbol of the divine presence. It had the very name of the Lord of Hosts. Its name and Jehovah was synonymous. "Bring up from thence the ark of God that is called by the name of the Lord of Hosts." — II Samuel 6:1-12.

This subject is the third in the series relating to national government, or adeptship on a large scale. Divine authority and divine adeptship are one and the same. The nearer divine the national intention, the more authority is vested in the nation and the nearer the nation comes to finally dictating terms to other nations.

Is there any nation with a diviner principle running through its networks than the one that insists that all men having been born free and equal they shall be preserved in freedom and equality? Is not this principle nearer the divine intention as touching mankind than any which makes chiefly for the defense of a king or the enlargement of a kingdom? "Which is broader in scope, "God save the king," or "God bless our nation?"

These lessons, commencing July 5, have meant to tell that some one nation or other has been allowed to have more to say than the others, up to date, about international matters, and that this subtly authoritative nation has ignored the common rights of common men.

For seventy years some underhanded policy had been operating against the ark of the Lord at the time when this lesson first applied to nations, B.C. 1042. And it comes up today as a positive proclamation that for seventy years some underhanded policy has been subtly winding its length and strength through that nation's fields, that has for its main purpose the common welfare of its whole people, male and female, black and white, old and young, foreign and native born.

That policy is clearly told by this section and has been plainly put by the others, but in a time of partisan feeling even an abstract principle seems to partake so much of agreeing with some system or method of action that it is deemed best to have people to draw their own inferences rather than explain principles so definitely that all must draw the same inference.

That policy, for the period of time represented in ancient literature by the number society, has been operating against the equal rights, and equal opportunities of modern nations, and is plainly told by the Bible sections.

One thing be certain of, however, and that is that methods count for nothing when divine principles are on the move. "It is not the man who is eloquent of tongue, but the man who is drunk with conviction" who convinces his fellow man. This is told in this Bible selection by the tumbling ark of the Lord on its rough journey from Baal-Judah to Jerusalem. It was getting along all right, though seemingly shaking and tottering, for the simple reason that it was headed for Jerusalem; but Uzzah undertook to brace it up. His method seemed to be the wise one, but the foolish method was getting on well enough, for that impetus of divine afflatus which gets to its destination anyway was behind it, "Uzzah put forth his hand to the ark of God and took hold of it, for the oxen shook it." — (Verse 6)

The ark had been neglected for seventy years by reason of the subtle reign of some axiom propounded by some adept who verily thought he was doing God service by sustaining it. That adept was, without doubt, Samuel, who made and unmade Saul with such definite power. His undermining axiom had been, "Rule or ruin." Under that subtle feeling he fixed his two sons into judgeship over Israel; and both these sons "turned aside after lucre, and took bribes." — (I Samuel 8:3)

So the ark which represented the people's rights had been steadily snubbed by all the heads of state for seventy years. But suddenly David appeared and headed the ark for Jerusalem. That is, started the ball of government rolling for the advantages of the people — the masses.

The Davidian Epoch

This Davidian epoch, so suddenly inaugurated after so many years of half protest against the Samuel type, was symbolized by taking the ark of the Lord in a new cart, "and Uzzah and Ahio, the sons of Abinadab, drove the new cart." (verse 3) These two men championed the people's cause. One had strength (Uzzah); the other had brotherly feeling (Ahio). One had a quantity of the stuff people adored in that age; the other had a fellow feeling for the masses, but none of the adorable stuff. The Bible concordance, explains this by telling the meaning of their names.

The whole story is the supernatural invention of whoever wrote the books of Samuel, and has for its purpose the straight information to our age as to how our government will get on in its new "cart," with its two new men, with the people's highest interest at heart.

One is going to use his adored stuff freely, thinking the good of the cause demands it and he is going to be so mistaken in his supposition that he will drop into oblivion. (Verse 7) "And the anger of the Lord was kindled against Uzzah, and God smote him there for his error; and there he died, by the ark of God."

In ancient literature the law of cause and effect is called the anger of God when it ends in pain, and the pleasure of the Lord when it ends in prosperity. It is as if we should say mathematics is angry when I say four minus two is three, and pleased when I say four minus two is two. Uzzah and his colleagues had agreed that the divine afflatus in the ark was its own defense and victory. Then let that afflatus attend to its own progress. It was not his business to help it on.

A great deal of misery has been endured by people trying to defend the truth, the right. The martyrs all fought for their principles, not what they called their God. So they suffered death and bruises. The actual fact is that a principle can take care of itself and everybody who espouses it, and, however tottering and trembling it may seem to be, it is certain to come up like a rock of phosphorous in the sea — a shelter and a lighthouse for all who see it. The Davidian spirit that is now rousing in the people is certainly a renewed interest in the rights of the masses.

There must have been some policy of nations winding its subtle darkness through all the affairs of modern times when such amazing differences can loom up as now expose themselves between class and class. It is not industry that counts. It is not integrity that weighs. Was it integrity of purpose that put the mayors, the Governors, the Presidents, and the Kings into their seats? Does industry count the little children in the mills anything by the side of the wide opportunities of the mill owner's young ones?

The Policy of Nations

What policy of nations has been winding in and out that the ark of the Lord, or the common chances of all the people, have been so long snubbed? And who are the "Uzzah and Ahio" who are to start up a "new cart" to carry to prosperity the nation at this time, one of whom the one with so much of the adored stuff of all nations abroad — shall make such an egregious blunder?

The Davidian spirit of interest in the whole people at once, that is now rousing itself, after a long period of hiding, shall conquer, after two experiences, according to this Bible lesson. After the first rousing, a shock; then a triumph. (Read verses 10 and 12). It is the same with individuals; and no nation shall be exempt from having some events and men who shall carry out the symbol in this chapter in some fashion.

For logic is logic, and events and men have an unvarying logic until they step out of the law of sequence.

The ark of the Lord bore the name of the Lord in David's time. Does one nation now bear the name of the Lord? "What one stands for unity, union, one? "In that day there shall be one Lord and his name one." That one is the best representative then, of the spirit of the times, and its prosperity or palsy is the decree for other nations, just as the ark which had the .same name as the Lord three thousand years ago represented the prosperity or palsy of all Israel.

The main point of the lessons of the coming six months is to be the divine authority which swings down through a man when he makes his own throneship, or original divinity, the principle object of his attention. And the influence which a small number of people will exert, without intending to do so, on a whole nation, to set its face toward Jerusalem, is to be continually mentioned. There is nobody so widely influential as he who knows the true God. And the true God is the "I AM" of each man — his own divine soul.

The attention of a man toward his own soul is always illustrated in the Bible by a journey toward Jerusalem. When the ark of the Lord traveled toward Jerusalem is it meant that a nation was interested in the soul nature, the soul ways of the people?

The soul is always equally majestic, equally intelligent, equally beautiful, in all people. Wherever there are great differences in intelligence and nobility there has been little or no attention toward the soul. In other words, the ark of the Lord has not been on the road toward Jerusalem, but stopping among the Philistines or at Baal-Judah. To be plainer, the heads of government have been like

Samuel's sons, or like Saul, all of whom had the rule or ruin and lucre- seeking mind.

The Souls of Men

But somebody has been attending to the soul of all men, as one man, by attending strictly to his own "I AM," naming it by the authoritative, dictating, all-victorious name, for there is the stir of some honest wing of interest in the rights of the people just now. There has been in the past a great talk about this interest, but now there is the stir of a genuine interest. Therefore, some dictating one has arisen; at whose pungent sentence some old measure shall lose its print and some new measure shall come into sight, with more equal chances for the people in its practice. A new adept is here in our midst.

"At that time shall Michael stand up, the great prince which standeth for the children of the people, and there shall be a time of trouble, such as never was since there was a nation." — Daniel 12:1

Daniel saw into our age and told it by pictures, exactly as the author of the Samuel books saw into it and told it by today's chapter on the journey of the ark.

David was troubled by the brother of Uzzah. It made him stop three months from managing the journey of the ark toward Jerusalem. But finally he got it there with gladness. (Verse 12) So, be not dismayed, says this lesson, by the strange blunder of somebody who is going to act straight against his once proclaimed principles, for he shall go into oblivion, but the rights of the people shall be maintained and prosperity shall rouse in gladness after his astonishing fiasco.

"For the elect's sake those days shall be shortened" in which trouble seems to reign; David had to wait only three months. Nobody has long to wait now. The days of long waiting for divine kindnesses to appear to individuals and nations are past. The command, "Be swift, my soul, to conquer," is promptly obeyed by the omnipotent soul.

As Jesus of Nazareth obeyed with alacrity in meek but mighty achievements, so, now, the same soul works swiftly for the redemption, the glory, the free glad life of each and all the people of the nation.

Prophecy is foretelling which the fulfillment keeps exact pace; else it is but a tiresome fable of some doubtful future. This prophecy keeps parallel with its fulfillments. The day has arrived when "while they are yet speaking" it shall come to pass.

Michael, in the spirit standing forth, does with his fiery garments sweep the winds of inspiration through the people with one accord, so that no longer can sophistries deceive them, but their open-eyed intelligence responds only to the divinest adeptship. Only to him that is inspired by the winds of the new age will any man of the new age listen. Behold, one maketh all things new.

Inter-Ocean Newspaper, July 19, 1896

LESSON IV

Purpose Of An Adept

II Samuel 7:4-16

An adept is one who can set currents of thought or will to going through the minds and wills of men and the men will do exactly according to those currents.

An adept of the Eastern type performs secretly. He is no orator, no writer, but in the secrecy of his chamber he sits and starts currents of operation to going as he wills.

An adept of the Western type makes himself visible and audible. He is an orator, a writer, a Governor of state, who, with tricks at speech or pen, catches the ears and hearts of his contemporaries, and they follow his biddings.

Some adepts are projective; they give forth such a quality from themselves that all the people who feel it begin to like it. Such adepts color a whole nation with their views. Voltaire projected in such a fashion his ideas throughout France. It was not till someone arose and proclaimed with the forcefulness of an adept, that Voltaire had no soul, that the almost indelible ink of Voltaire's views began to fade out of France.

Some adepts are magnetic; they draw to themselves from their contemporaries a feeling exactly like their own, concerning themselves. We have a notable example in America to represent this type. He felt so strongly that he was a great character, a great man that thousands upon thousands agreed with him. They placed him high. He did not however, know what to do in his high place, or with his high place.

Solomon discovered, 1015 B.C., that he himself was of this order of adeptship and was afraid that when he had been raised into the high seat where such men always get, that he should not know what to do in it or with it. So he worked earnestly to focalize that all-wise spirit in his heart. He did fairly well in melding wisdom with greatness. His contemporaries added the opinion that he was wise to his own opinion to that effect. They added the opinion that he was great to his own opinion of the same.

David's Influence

David, the father of Solomon, was of the projective order of adeptship. He thrust his indelible print on mind and will in every direction. To this day David's color tinges all religious feeling and rouses all men's emulation.

The adept who sets up his own current and succeeds, either at making people move around to suit him, or praise him greatly, must reach the limit of his power some time, somewhere. He gets softening of the brain at middle age, or driveling senility in the face and eyes of his contemporaries. Sometimes he makes a terrible blunder. His blunders will always be equal in stature with his force. Daniel Webster is a good illustration.

Jesus of Nazareth discovered that he was an adept of both the projective and magnetic order. He saw that by the sweep of his eyes over an army they would cringe. He saw that by the mere consent of his will to the idea of his human greatness he could be a King. He found that by letting loose the last little bit of his personal influence he could have ruled the world so much better than Nero, Queen Victoria, or President Cleveland? Today's lesson explains. Its texts declare why. They are to be found in II Samuel 7:4-16.

The golden text hints it: "In thee, O Lord, do I put my trust." The plain rendering of the whole lesson is that there is an untouchable, unalterable, impartial will that is not identified with anybody's currents of operation no matter how shrewd or forceful his personal adeptship may be; and that nobody can see or feel the splendor of the works of this impartial will till he or she stops projecting or materializing on his or her own account.

Each man, each woman has the personal force to set the currents going or coming. All have personal forces. Jesus had extra amounts of this. He would not use any of it. The people of this generation would adjudge any man a fool who declined to go in and win with such a bottle of mystic and mighty energy in his possession as Jesus had.

Providing Up an Idea

Almost all the metaphysics books and magazines of this age are devoted to the description of processes for providing up an idea with either projective or magnetic powerfulness. They say: "If you want to feel the thrills of a happy life, you must repeat in silence the word 'life', believe in the presence of life, breathe into your nostrils the common air as though it were life, eat your bread as though it were life, eat your bread as though you were eating life, sleep as though you rested on life," etc. They say the same about health. Then they find that those who practice this formula faithfully do either give an aroma fresh life and health everywhere or arouse fresh life and health within themselves.

Jesus was willing to be a fool, a nobody, that the wonderful country and glorious people seen by the Impartial Will, that never yet was mixed up with personal wills, might be visible to him unclouded, unveiled by his personal imaginations, wishes, or forcefulness. If that was his stupidity, make the most of it. Whose great, so-called force of character, printing its determinations on the age in which it flourished, has brought so much hope, light, freedom from evil, repose in divinity as his?

Has Julius Caesar's, Pompey's, Napoleon's, Jay-Gould's, or Gladstone's?

Today's lesson brings up David as one who foreran Jesus in the discovery that, if he would cease from projecting his own wishes and wills, he would see something going on about him that would have just the right influence on his daily life and on the destiny of nations to come. This lesson is the fourth in the series of national events. All that it means must be applied to the country's fate and duty. So must all the coming lessons mean, from now on to the last lesson in December of this year.

There are some people who now know enough to keep still, and have the Almighty alone for their comrade. They know enough not to write or speak or think what they know. They know enough to let the Omnipotent will in whose substance all is finished print its colors and figures in plain sight of their eyes, and yet they hold their peace. And their holding their peace at sight of the finished things of the kingdom around them makes them a new type of adepts on the earth; such as never appeared since Jesus saw the same country and interfered nothing of his own wish, with Rome, or Gaul, or Greece. They pass for nobodies — nothing, so unforceful are they. Thus they are adepts of neither the protective nor magnetic type. They are forerunners of the actual Jesus type, just as David and Nathan mentioned in this chapter: "And it came to pass that night that the word of the Lord came unto Nathan, saying, Go and tell my servant, David, I took thee from the sheep-cote, from following the sheep, to be ruler over Israel. And I was with thee withersoever thou wentest, and have cut off all thine enemies out of thy sight, and have made thee a great name, like unto the name of the great men that are in the earth." (Verses 4-10)

Arm in Arm with the Almighty

This wonderful comrade of David, whose name was the unspeakable name was let by David, so far as he could keep himself out of the question, to have his own divine way, daily, and the consequence was that by contact with such a comrade David got some of his characteristic and qualities. The man who can get himself seen arm-in-arm with Rothschild's can get unlimited credit at any bank. David, by walking arm-in-arm with the Almighty, was a vanquisher of opposition withersoever he walked. Emerson, in a moment of revelation, said that whoever should have the Omnipotent for his comrade, walking with no other friends, leaning on no other banker, should have honor and fortune come to him without any effort on his own part.

Now the book we call the Bible is all written over with this Emersonian revelation. This story of David is one of its accounts of the same. "Yet who hath believed its report, or to whom hath the arm of such a God been revealed?" cried Isaiah, in his age, and crieth this lesson to our age.

Our Nation has a few on hand who are certain that the influence of heavenly things is on the present crisis. These few lean hard on the arm of their only comrade: the Lord of Hosts is his name. By some strange movements of theirs they walk alone save companioned by the Almighty. At no point in their career are they in touch with their contemporaries either by projective or magnetic adeptship on a large or on a small scale. They must have the Almighty to their friend or go under.

If you tell them of your prowess in hunting and fishing they cannot cheer you on by approval. If you tell them of your power over men and women by the force of your personal presence they cannot praise you or fall in with your opinion, though it will be well strengthened by the opinions of the multitude. If you boast of your bags of gold and silver, which some adepts have printed with values so distinctly that nations and principalities and cities and Kings are staggered into agreement therewith, they are not awed by you. They know of a kingdom where nobody hurts or kills. They know of a kingdom where one is as lovely and cheered in his life as another. They lean on the arm of its King. They feel their feet sandaled in beauty walking through the unseen streets of a city of light, where they do not rank children great who own gold mines and small who toil in the same. They feel the grasses of some sweet pastures, the sounds of a glad-sounding shore where they neither buy nor sell nor hoard nor give, for it is an impartial will that there reigns. They rest on the hand of this will.

Saw Into the Future

There must be some such people among us now; else this chapter could not be the international subject of study, today. And it is these people who herald the hastening in of the Jesus Christ actual. David and Nathan saw ahead a thousand years. They felt the mountains quake under the tread of one to come who made himself of none account and no weight to earth. They saw further. They saw that he, the weightless one, should himself herald the coming into sight at some still distant day from his own of multitudes on multitudes who should neither buy nor sell nor hurt nor kill nor govern nor teach.

They saw ahead a thousand years into the daily walk of one whose only comrade was the Almighty. They saw him making no time between his presence and the mighty works of raising the dead, healing the sick, lifting up the broken hearted. They saw further. They saw ahead of him into a day when there should be no time between the need of a nation and the supply of a nation.

They saw nation after nation lifting up its adepts, called Kings, governors, presidents, into high seats to legislate on money and commerce and learning, in such fashions as should year by year hurry the poor to be poorer and the rich to be richer with an eye among the high seated ones to pity and no arm to save.

They touch with prophetic glance the page of the year 1896, when the harvest of the governorship, legislation, and protectorship of all kings, all potentials should be ripe.

The unfortunate masses are taught that the learned ones, the richly born ones, have and always will have the right to lord it over them, mete out to them their wages and print on the gold and silver found in the ground such values as they should ordain. This is the state of affairs. This is the harvest of time over whose fields the long vista'd eyes of David threw their glances three thousand years ago.

And walking close to the bowed millions David and Nathan saw one with countenance like unto the Son of Man. They saw some of the betrayed multitudes lifting up their eyes to this comrade. They saw them rise up with a shout. They saw how the bowed down millions caught the cause of the shout of their neighbors and rose with them as one man, and the reign of the learned richly born over the world was ended. The poor had the gospel preached unto them and nevermore the sound of child-labor as ordained by the learned and richly born should be heard. The world had heard of its comrade and no more should it be governed by the stamps and superscriptions on metals found in the dirt as decreed by the un-Christly adepts of earth.

Seek ye out the book of our God and read. No one shall miss sight of his mate, this comrade, this friend, this provider, this God. Whosoever shall first lean hard enough on this comrade with the omnipotent arm to find himself independent of the owners of the mills, the ships, the railroads, the stores shall shout with joy so resounding that the very meaning of this noise shall be communicable. "For the ransomed of the Lord shall come with singing." "And the Lord shall come with the shout." And the day of redemption is nigh when the people ask and the Princes heed not."

And the house of every man shall be established. The Kingdom shall not faint wherein he sees all alike awake to the knowledge of eternal, changeless, all powerful comrade — the Lord of Hosts is his name.- (Verses 13-16)

David in Jerusalem, seeing the days ahead, sent out a word of cheer. Nathan took up the cry, and passed it on over the wings of the flying centuries. Jesus fulfilled their foresight with sight. His sight has now finished its course.

There surely is no more need now to exercise the mind and the will to bring to pass great events now, when the day has broken on the mountain tops of the earth that plainly shows the mystery and might of the unfailing comrade and the bountiful, tender ways of the kingdom not made with hands, eternal heaven set on the earth, in its midst, everywhere.

This Section teaches that all those men whose hand, is to have it all his own way, and nothing and nobody can hinder him. The day of all personal will has entered its last night.

That which happens is to lift up the eyes of the masses to know who and what it is that protects, defends, prospers, exalts them. It is not the same old system, but a new one — new as the temple David began in Jerusalem, new as the nation he founded, new as the vision he had of a people walking as one man, alone with the Almighty One, leading on no prince or corporation, dependent on no man's will.

There is no man strong enough, to stem the tide. There is no will can combat it. No army of wills can hide it. The throne of the new system is being set up by the hand of the friend of David.

For, "moreover I will appoint a place for my people, and will plant them, that they dwell in a place of their own, and be moved no more; neither shall the children of wickedness afflict them anymore."

The Inter Ocean Newspaper, July 26, 1896

Lesson V

Individual Emancipation

II Samuel 9:1-13

"The bird that soars on highest wing
Builds on the ground her lowly nest;
And she that doth most sweetly sing
Sings in the shade when all things rest."

DAVID'S KINGDOM

The story of David's kingdom in the far past has been preserved to our age because of its inspiration of information concerning our age with its chaotic states of under-trodden millions and exalted few.

David was a shepherd boy, whose lifelong habit it had been to recognize the presence of an all-powerful comrade forever near him. He never praised himself as "great David," but praised the greatness of this comrade, whose majesty he adored. The very name of this ever-present friend was capable of nerving David with mettle enough to conquer armies of enemies.

"Thou comest unto me with spear, and sword, and shield, but I come unto thee in the name."

In the strength generated by this name David took Jebus and made it Jerusalem. He took the people of Jebus and made them his people. He roused the spirit of patriotism in a small and disordered country to such white heat that for their city and its golden temple all Israel stood ready to die. He found an old system flourishing, under whose legalized practices the few who had been favored by some accident of opportunity were keeping in abeyance the many who had been unfortunate enough to have been born in the ranks. This had made the masses distrust the protecting kindness of God, and thus religion was at a low ebb. Syndicates and corporations had grown up under that system till, when David took the reins of government, the multitudes had nothing to live on, while the minority had all there was.

Source of David's Power

The might and prowess of David's mind had all been gendered by continual remembrance of the Most High One, who kept him company. He had learned the secret of conquering every opposition by resting all his weight on the arm of his ever-present friend. He had learned the secret of brilliant statesmanship by keeping his mind always at the practice of acknowledging that itself was nothing, but the friend was all. He had found out that the cheapest and foolishest of men may be grand and intelligently taking constant notice of the ever-present friend. He had found that no one needs any co-operation of a company of men and women, or even of one man or one woman, from the time he discovers the tremendous capacity and ability of the ever-present friend. He found that as by the draught of a lodestone all objects come to rest in its strength, so to the God-championed soul all the nations gather to do homage.

At the time when this lesson opens David, the sheep boy, had been the wise king of all Israel for several years. He had harmonized the split parties in his kingdom by altering the laws under whose shades such dissensions had grown up. He had organized the men into battalions, headed by well-tried champions of national rights. He had gathered the singers into choirs led by ardent lovers of the King of heaven. He had selected a cabinet of men, of whom it was written, that their counsel was "as if a man had inquired at the oracle of God."

Ignored Old Rules

He had utterly ignored the rule of his predecessors in the throne, and the predecessors of former cabinet officers, which had its directions clearly indicated, exactly as in our day, to wit:

"That good old rule, the simple plan,

That they should take who have the power And they should keep who can."

He had, by acquaintance with the all befriending heart, come to have a warm and merciful heart toward the lowliest creatures. He had himself felt the teeth of those men who had not warmed and quickened their hearts at the heart of the universe. He had seen how, but for the heart warmth of the walkers of God, this world would be but a cage of hyenas. He had caught from on high the secret of salvation from men and their deeds the secret of grandeur in self. He was not afraid of anybody or anything in all the world. He had seen himself saved from the wrath of a King, the spite of armies, the clinches of starvation by the rich and glorious heart of his secret friend. So, there, at the height of his prosperity, he begins to look about for something that needs heart's kindness. He finds Mephibosheth, lame in both feet, son of his dead friend, Jonathan, II Samuel 9:1-13. Now, Mephibosheth of ancient Jewry comes up on today's register, to notify us where the laboring classes are standing. Jonathan had loved these people. He, by loving David twenty years before, had loved these people, for David was a man of the people.

David was a heart of merciful friendliness everywhere. Kings and Princes felt it; the poverty-stricken son of Jonathan, lame in both feet, should feel it, too.

Lame in both feet! If there was ever anything lame in both feet it is the wage-earners of the world, as it is now careering with its fashion and combine, its bank and its factory government. Panic and famine for the masses, splendor and millions to hoard, at headquarters! This is Mephibosheth, 1896. Therefore, this lesson repeats the July 5 on the promise that truly, truly, there is now a friend in sight under whose wise administration the past practices must cease. And, verily, that which transpires very soon, in the leading Nation on earth, must transpire in every kingdom, for things are done on the international plan now. The whole earth is involved in everything that happens now to the nation which has for its purpose the equal chances of all its inhabitants.

Jerusalem of old, with David as King, was prototype of the whole earth today, with one nation teaching lessons to all its Kings. He who can read David's career wisely can read the prophecy of this age wisely.

Mephibosheth is well aware of his inferiority, caused by his unequal chances. "He bowed himself, and said, 'What is thy servant?' But David, the King, close friend of the Omnipotent Kindness, bade him stand up and come into his house, where he would soon forget his past, and be cured of his lameness.

The Bible teaches that this shall be true in a wider sense than by the uncommonly gallant administration of the incoming man of our Nation. It hints all the time at some miraculous appearing, some unprecedented event, as taking place at some point of time which David's action with Mephibosheth symbolizes, and which the incoming man is herald of.

Every Bible section is true on the plane where it is accepted. If on a mental plane, it is true that every individual on earth is about to raise up a new idea of kindliness to help the weaker side of his nature. It will mean, on that plane, that everybody falters in some particular, but his new idea will rouse his courage in that particular. But the Bible is a deeper book than that. It takes nations of men and shows them what is happening. It takes the soul of man and exhibits glory. It strikes into the unspoken and the untaught. It tells of things to be revealed of which no man hath yet tasted. It tells of a different judgment seat, from which all men are to decide matters. It describes the time and the thoughts of the world just before men, the world over, are to change their base of judgment and criterion for action. It says that the change of judgment in man shall be sudden, in a moment, in the twinkling of an eye. It shall be what has been hoped for, but hardly expected, just as Mephibosheth's hardly expected happiness suddenly sprang upon him.

The Bible tells of this time of our own Nation when a well-patronized, well honored system has caroused with the inhabitants; thereof till they are getting nearly as lame in both feet as the wage-earners of Russia. It also tells of a deplorable discouragement in the minds of all men. Then it tells of a sudden uplifting. But do not think the Bible stops at those prophecies. It strikes into some deeper uplifting, some higher arising, some heartier comfort than a good national ruler or a wise, new idea. It touches upon the wonderful words of Jesus Christ concerning the sudden appearance of the Comforter on the whole earth, the Holy Ghost, who shall teach us all, even the shabbiest, the lamest footed of us, how to be one with the Friend walking forever by our side, how to be as wise as the Friend, how to be as competent as the Friend, how to be as independent as the Friend.

That is told as Mephibosheth eating at the table of David, who was one with the friend; it is told by the saying of Jesus, "Behold, I stand at the door and knock, if any man will open the door I will come in and sup with him." "I and the Father are one."

All the world of metaphysicians may describe the glorious idea which is to swing in at the opening gates of this era. All the world of philosophers may speculate of the soon coming of a new force to the knowledge of men. All the world of religion may preach of David as forerunning Jesus, and Jesus as coming in the clouds of a new healing light, the Messiah of a future millennium. Each will find the Bible chapters a comfort and an information on the plane where they are taken. This section of II Samuel 9:1-13, asks: "Where are you walking? With whom are you talking? What do you expect?"

High above the mountain tops of the highest thoughts that have ever swung their golden censors dwelleth in unthought-of kindness, the One of whom these lessons speak to the nations. Low down below the deeps of the profoundest speculations that have ever rolled their dazzling chariots dwelleth in unspoken rest the One of whom these lessons chant to the world. Nearer then the tenderest winds of the divinest religions that has ever wrapped its healing wings around life's laming ways is the One, all sweetness, all strength, all kingly power, to whom these lessons point.

He who knoweth this mighty One can understand the flights of the archangels and the songs of heavenly cherubim, but to him these entrancing wonders are not more dear and near than the sound of the fearless lambs in the pastures of the incoming land holders. To him the knowledge of the ways of the eternal stars is not more precious than the knowledge that on all the earth the inhabitants shall never say "I am sick," any more, the people shall never weep any more, they shall hunger no more, neither for the knowledge of God nor for bread.

And to him the hunger of the underfed in the pens of the King-made nations is equally important with the nations hunger for God. He shall know that while ever there is hunger for bread there must be hunger for God. And that, while ever there is hunger for bread in a city, there, there is no man knows his God. No man walks at all with the Omnipotent Comrade if into, his sight a single hungry or maimed thing ever gets and goes away in the same state.

David, 3,000 years ago, gave an object lesson to presidents and princes for all time, when he picked up Mephibosheth.

But David could not have been noble, generous, magnanimous, to Saul's grandson the dangerous rival for his throne, had he not been the bosom comrade and faithful adorer of the friend that sticketh closer than a brother, the Majestic, Eternal One.

Inter-Ocean Newspaper, August 2, 1896

Lesson VI

The Almighty Friend

II Samuel 10:8-19

This day's Bible lesson gives a violent illustration of how success always lies in the track of one who leans on that invisible but almighty comrade forever accompanying each one of earth's children.

The plane on which David expected championship was the roughest of planes, viz., material warfare with spears and swords and shields, in hand to hand blood drawing. He expected his God to walk by his side and nerve his soldiers' arms and hearts with overpowering strokes. And his God did exactly that. The Syrians and Ammonites fell down and acknowledged themselves terribly beaten. They hung their heads, and said David was something superhuman.

Of course this international section, Second Samuel, 10:8-19, now applies to the United States in particular, and to all other nations in general. For as David had the best conceptions of the rights of the people in his age, 1040 B.C., so this western Nation of ours has the best conceptions of the rights of the people now. This is not boasting that wither David's or this national sentiment is wholly wise or beneficent, but only that compared with other kings of his time David was ahead, and compared with national sentiment in other countries ours is ahead.

Thus we may expect some mighty evidence about these days, of the victorious quality of the substantial One upon whom somebody, or some party, or some band of people in our country, is leaning. They, or he, or she, whether one alone, or many banded together, can count on the battle coming out in their favor. And, as they are most interested for the great multitude so there is to be the greatest good to the greatest number by the success of their swords and spears.

Lesson from the Life of David

This is all made unquestionably evident by the way David rose up and used Joab and Abishai, two determined generals, as aids de camp in this great effort to throw down the two then flourishing hordes of enemies to the people. Joab was patriotic. Abishai was patriotic enough if somebody would only prod him up to it. "Be of good courage," said Joab to him, "And let us play the enemies for the sake of our own people and for the cities of our God; and the Lord do that which seemeth to him good." (Verse 12) This was sufficient prodding up for Abishai, and then they took their two respective wings of David's splendid army and tore Syrians and Ammonites to pieces. (Verse 14)

The warfare of Paul, nearly 1,100 years later, was more elusive, ethereal, unsubstantial, but just as victorious. His battle cry was: "For we wrestle not against flesh and blood, but against principalities, against powers, against the rulers of darkness of this world, against spiritual wickedness in high places." His triumphant shout was: "I have fought a good fight, I have finished my course, I have kept the faith; henceforth there is laid up for me a crown of righteousness." His crown was to be as elusive and intangible as the enemies he had fought. Nothing is more untempting to human beings than a crown of righteousness, unless they have, like Paul, transferred their fighting from the material to the mental plane.

Once our Christian soldiers had a Satan and his angels, invisible mostly, but coming often enough into light to convince the soldiers of their actual existence, John Wesley and Martin Luthe2 had visits from Satan, and held conversations with him. The later Christian soldiers called the enemies to man by other names. They said it was the principle of evil with all its laws. Some of them called it personal magnetism, making it a state of mind, with a circulating atmosphere of harm.

Whatever name they called it by made no difference to their victories. Leaning on the arm of their mighty Deliverer, they either fought with mind and tongue, or with guns and fires their very successful battles.

Mrs. Hettie Green says that she leans on her God and he shows her how to make stupendous deals, which always profit herself. The church fathers, leaning on the arm of their God, burned John Rogers at the stake. He could not lean on his God hard enough to get out of their clutches, but this lesson is put down in the ember of history to inform us that if he expected his God to get him loose he would have done so, and the church fathers would have cringed and crawled like the Ammonites and Syrians of this chapter.

David bore down with his whole weight on the presence of one with omnipotent energy. He bore his whole mind's weight on the presence of one with omniscient shrewdness, intelligence, quickness in judgment. He knew enough to set Joab over one wing of his army and Abishai over another. These two together made a pair of skilled brave, invincible, wily, unscrupulous, cruel generals. It is astonishing how strange are the means employed by those who, like David, have to perform with their hands and guns and ballots and money, or like Paul, with their thoughts and will and personal magnetism, in order to defeat their opponents. Everything rises up from everywhere to help them.

Now, this is all well on the fight plane. It works well. You can succeed with your gun if you shoot while you lean hard on the omnipotent, omniscient friend to nerve and direct the shooting. You can use your money to the cleverest advantage if you lean hard on the omnipotent, omniscient friend to direct your handling thereof, like the rich woman above mentioned.

Another Road to Success

But there is still another plane on which we can succeed. It is the nofight plane. And on this plane, too, everything in creation rises up from ambush everywhere, from stones and snakes to men and money, to help us to be successful.

If you set out to live on this plane, the wily and unscrupulous serve you. The benevolent and merciful serve you. The forces of the universe conspire for your success, happiness, prosperity.

All the Bible stories point to this fightless, noncontentious plane as the divinest plane, the most ennobling, the most intelligencing.

Peace on earth — peace, peace. Not the peace won by fighting sin, wrong, evil; not the peace won by guns, swords, money; but the peace of God, that passeth understanding. While there is any expectation that the divine comrade will make us successful against some enemies arrayed against us, we are liable to unhappy days and deep glooms. We are liable to err. David committed a certain blunder very much resembling the way some prince and emperors of our own Christian day act. He mourned and gloomed like the wailings of our modern reformers who are dragging people out of the ditches of sin.

But on the no-fight plane they sorrow no more. Not looking for any evil to pound and smash and annihilate, they find none and thus there is nothing to groan over.

God Always Ready to Help

If there is one mighty presence in this universe so gracious and competent and indulgent that he is willing to spear and sling for David, to think and magnetize for Paul, to invest for H. Green, shall he not work as grandly and mightily in behalf of the peaceable, fightless me?

Shall not the wily snakes in the forests peaceably rise up to clear my path? They are my Joab and Abishai. Shall not the invincible gold of the country, the plenteous silver, unscrupulous, cruel, treacherous though they have been made, in their innocence, arrange themselves to protect my journey? They are Joab and Abishai for me. Every move made to hurt shall profit me. But I need not move, I need not speak, I need not reply. I need know nothing whatsoever of how the armies of disadvantage to me are arraying themselves. That is, if I am on the non-fight, peaceable, silent plane, I lean as confidently on this indulgent, all-powerful comrade as an impartial benefactor to all as David did, as Paul did, as H. Green does, all for their own advantage and to nobody else's. I need not be thinking that I must exercise my thoughts like battle horses, nor my hands and friends in my behalf. What does not rise up and run forward, sway and compel everything for my sake, without any of my assistance, is not mine. This is providing I am on the fightless plane, leaning on the arm of that equal friend of every man.

All the Bible lessons on this globe are enjoying a fight of some sort. On the patriotic battle fields, pounding with gun handles, cutting with sabers, the North and the South fought each other. The war cry of all was: "Strike, strike, strike, for God and your native land. Anything so you strike,"

Salvation Is Emancipation

On the salvation-from-sin field it is, "Strike for your liberty from the blackest sin that clutches you. Rise up in your opposition and down the temptation."

On the non-fight field the Lord God omnipotent sets all opponents aside and we are not aware there have been any. On the non-fight field the mighty deliverer sets the temptation out of our way and we never even knew that we had come near one.

"Lead us not into temptation," was the command of Jesus the peaceable to his great friend. "Deliver us from evil, both as we believe and as we can feel," he continued. He said that such heresy to the fight doctrine would set the fighters to going afresh, but no fear need stir, nor should stir those who had begun to lean on the over indulgent friend in the expectation of immunity from discord.

"Fear not." This is the secret subconscious reason why the golden text of today reads: "The Lord is my light and my salvation; whom shall I fear?" This lesson declares that David was not an absolutely perfect example of leaning on the great friend as one to lift us out and up by himself, for he cut and slashed his enemies like a splendid soldier that he was to show how strong he could be with such saving nerves as his friend had woven together in him. This lesson hints that Paul was not an absolutely perfect example of leaning on the great friend, for he never left off his injunctions to be wrestling against something and using the heavenly comrade to forward our undertakings.

This lesson points with its subtle; secret, but deathless finger toward some use to put the heavenly one unto besides directing slings, stones, money bags, or mind with and will in our own behalf.

It sings with a never varying charm under the twang of the story of bows and stones and money and mind, and its song it forever and forever about some majestic sweetness, some glory and loveliness far beyond the story of using the wonderful soul, the heavenly One, to whip and scourge our neighbors for our sakes. Something rolls and chants through this bold illustration our committee selects for our investigation grander than heroic battling against enemies. It is the victorious chariot-wheels of fightless peace. Every sound from this story that cannot be hushed is melodious as the songs and harps of singing cherubims.

The mother snatches her happy child from the flames and our friend snatches us from the pains of a wrestling world full of flaming zeal. Like as one whom his mother comforteth so is this secret song the sound of the feet of the new sons of light.

Inter-Ocean Newspaper, August 9, 1896

Lesson VII

Missing

LESSON VIII

Individual Emancipation

II Samuel 15:1-12

The title of this lesson is, according to the outer interpretation of the Bible chapter, "Absalom's Rebellion." The title of it according to the secret or inner science is "Individual Emancipation." To the first sight or first reading of the texts it seems as if Absalom's wily plotting against David's kingdom were a terrible misfortune to David, but to the second sight it shows the sweet surgery of the Omnipotent Kindness working in his behalf.

The prayer of David, which was not so much a pleading beggar's attitude of mind as it was a direct commandment to the Heavenly Will, has not its practical fulfillment. For, notice, every personal trait we have has it counterpart in some personality we are associated with.

David's command to Omnipotent Kindness, or the Heavenly Will, had been, "Cleanse thou me from secret faults." Absalom represented one of David's partly recognized secret faults. So, in the day when that particular fault began to dissolve, Absalom began to prepare a net for himself. The young man verily thought he was exalting himself by seductively talking to the adherents, constituents, and friends of David. Especially did he think so when he saw those friends rallying around himself and trying to pick flaws in David.

"But thy star is mine, Napoleon," said Josephine, and when Josephine was not prospered Napoleon landed on St. Helena. Thus might David have said to Absalom, "The star is mine, my boy," for when anything struck David, with his eyes fixed on high, the rebound of the striker must be sharp, final, unhinderable.

The experience for the king of the United States is set out for immediate transaction by this chapter being now chosen. It represents some wily demagogue working upon the supporters of the principles of our government to set them against public sentiment. The king of the United States is public sentiment, or the people's will. Somebody thinks that he can flatter, cajole, buy, threaten, or in some other way arrange with political leaders to stand as a sold phalanx, to speechify, and promise, till the people's will is undermined, hidden, forgotten, made of no account. (II Samuel 15:2)

"But the star is mine," the people may safely say. The victory is with the silent chord in the breast of the multitude. Let them keep as still as they please, let them listen to the speeches, the honest oratory of the well-paid, well-fed platform haranguers, they will know what governmental action has always preceeded panics, and what national act has always caused hard times. They know how brainy highwaymen have secured the revolvers of the present with which they hold up the masses, making them skip with glee when they open their shoe shops and cotton-mills, and droop with fear when they close up the same.

There is nothing but defeat for Absalom. That is, there is nothing but defeat for the orators. The silent David chord in the breast of the multitude is about to express itself. But at present the Absalom oratory, schools of political science, efforts to equate the mind with the dinner pails must have full swing.

David has made one wretched blunder, he has put in one headstrong characteristic as ruler over him, and Absalom thinks his silent meditations must mean easy defeat. But he is bravely mistaken. The simple hearted, trusting multitude made one wretched blunder through believing what they were told. But they will not make that same blunder again. They are keener minded, better posted. They have prayed in too many starving homes. The silent mind of the multitude is king. Meantime, let Absalom ride around with posters and money and well-groomed beard. (II Samuel 15:1-12)

Thus closely does the campaign of 1896 copy the campaign of 1022 B.C. Each side can regard the other as Absalom, but only one side is really Absalom. The multitude with the rusty dinner pails is not deceived, but it says very little.

The prayer of man is his way of attending to the Divine presence. In this age we were, as a unit, driven by circumstances, all over our country, to attending the Divine presence with prayers. They were petitions, commands, humble beggings, noble appeals, all sorts of ways of laying hold of the Author of life. The fruits of such attentions are nigh. The active half cause of the misery of the multitude is about to be cut off right in the splendor and strength of its riches. But there are no outward signs that his stay could not set. Did not Absalom seem to have it all his own way? So, a certain side of the controversy seems now to have things all its own way.

There is a strange waking up all over the world. Some hitherto hidden wisdom in the breasts of the masses seems breaking out like a light seems to have a force with it that no kings or queens or governors appointed by men can resist or gainsay. "Arise, shine, for thy lighteth every man that cometh into the world." Its march is peace on earth, but whosoever striketh at it himself shall be Absalom. To be sure, the people are dirty if she had been kicked and cuffed since her cradle and had never had the kind of surroundings that refine and beautify. To be sure, the people are ignorant, but so would President Harper be ignorant if he had been spit upon, fed on onions, and kept in a factory, or at a hand-organ, under the lash hunger and sickness ever since his birth in the flesh.

It has been the privilege and duty of those who have had the externals of human existence in rich beauty to make a way for those who have had no beauty in human existence. But they would not. So the sandpapering of the masses has gone on till the veneers of dirt and ignorance themselves are thin as tissue veils, through which the spirit of the all wise Christ is now giving signs of shining. The secret light in the hearts of the dirty and the ignorant is the light of God. How Jesus loved to say: "I came to the sinners. I care nothing for presentations at courts, seats in halls of learning. I glory in waking the light in the breasts of the dirty and ignorant. Shine forth, light of God, through the dark scowls of hunger, humiliation, human passions! Shine, light of the world cannot die! I am the light. I and the light are one. Wake, sons of God! Stand upright on your feet! The light is able to make you stand. I can give you a voice and wisdom, so that no man shall be able to gainsay or resist."

It has been nearly two thousand years since the voice of the awakener of the light in man shook the hills of Jerusalem with its great tones. Kings have risen and waned, flaunting the rags of unpaid toil across the faces of the people Jesus loved; universities have reared their marble walls and fallen into disuse scorning the light in the secret places of the scullions who served them, but the light they scorned, which Jesus saw shining as eternal stars of his father's countenance in the scullion's stupid eyes is not quenched. Its breaking forth is his final achievement.

Though the darkness hides the light of man through age on age its sleepless splendor shall spring up and break forth, burning the ignorance of Russian serfs and American factory slaves at one and the same instant. The science of Jesus Christ is the science of the lightning. One deepest scheme after another of the rulers of this world shall operate — nay, has operated — to seem to bury the light of the human swarms out of sight more and more. But look at David who stood for the light of the world 3,000 years ago. Look at plotting Absalom. Young, handsome, richly equipped, haughty, David seemed likely to be utterly quenched by him. The airs gathered in darkening globules four years of electric gloom for David to all appearances, but those four years were the surgical sharpening of the lightning knife for David's riddance of his fault and its embodiment.

Something in David's daily life was at variance forever with the beaming influence of the Divine one toward whom his eyes were cast. It was his marriages. It was his children. Thus all this surgery worked painfully along the family life, though always toward cutting them off for his personal freedom.

On the line where we are always in opposition to the beaming wisdom from the high God, we get our pains at the surgery of the gathered lightning if trouble does its work. It is true, we get freer and freer through our pains, but there is no need of pain. All pain represents some personal action of mind and body defying, either consciously or unconsciously, the steady meaning of the divine light forever shining down upon us from one God, forever shining through us from the light that lighteth every man that cometh into the world.

It is certain that whatever shall now seem so grievous to each of us, as some hitherto trusted person begins his schemes in open earnest against us, is the surgery of kindness setting us free from secret fault and open enemy, but it is not the straight offering of our persistent fault as a gift to the all-cleansing God. (see last Sunday's sermon). As David never knew that his marriages and his children crossed against the light, this one surgical operation, making ready in this chapter, did not set him finally free.

With Absalom's treachery the family inconsistency loomed into sight. With Absalom's sudden death the great light near David's face broke out, the city was saved to his wise rulership, his throne was his own. But Nathan told him the sword should never depart from his house. And it never did. The sword shall never depart from the house of any man while with his prayers he faces the divine presence, and with his actions he goes against it. The sword shall never depart from any nation while its people face the divine presence in prayers, and with their actions go against the influence of that presence. Individuals and nations go together. Whatever one man experiences or knows is generally felt and known.

As Jesus perceived the light gleaming through the eyes of the blindest cripple, he saw him perpetually holding up one personal characteristic as a blind, to return again and again for divine surgery till he laid it down.

But he saw us all, one man and one nation, all people and all nations, simultaneously catching the name of our blind and offering it for the fires of the sun of wisdom to dissolve. "Then shall thy light break forth as the morning and thy health shall spring forth speedily."

It was thought, by David, to be a virtue all his own conduct. So some virtue we pride ourselves upon is and has been the cause of our needing painful surgery to set us step by step one degree nearer and nearer toward our own great light. David ran his virtue so hard that at one point it became acknowledged vice. Then he took it in hand. So each individual now runs some virtue so far that at one point it is vice. For, as the farthest point east is west, and the farthest point west is east, so extended righteousness is vice.

"Be not righteous overmuch," says the Bible. (Eccl. 7:16) But at the vice point man and nation feels the sting as David's story teaches.

This applies to the ignorant masses of today. At the deepest point of ignorance their light is nearest. At the extremest touch of poverty they are nearest the Divine Beneficence, and its mighty skill is nearest teaching them a new spring to make on the world its governorship over them.

As the world stands how well has the learning thereof managed with the multitudes? Let the learning of the world answer. Then let the ignorance of the world answer. As it stands, how well have its rich kings and governing potentates handled the masses? Let the rich kings answer. Then let the poverty-stricken answer. It is at this question and answer point that the day's lesson finds the whole world. With David's particular crossing against the influence of the Divine light always kept up, of course, the swords were always handling his affairs. Yet no treacherous beloved or open hater ever took away his throne. He stands thus as holding his own against painful odds. Under the candle flame of the light of this moment we see why he had painful odds.

With our particular personal crossing against the influence of the divine light we have also had the sword of adversity to lop off the disadvantages against us as individuals and nations. Under some light to be thrown on our life somebody can see for us, either in the far future or right now, what we might let go of to go free from adversity, both as individual and nation. This lesson does not read as if anybody or any nation would let go of the crossing blind he is holding so rigidly as his virtue against the melting influence offering itself as his friend today from on high. "Go in peace," said David to Absalom (verse 9), feeling the sweet kindness of Jehovah shining on his heart. But still he rigidly held onto his wives and concubines.

"My face is set froward the Absolute I Am. I will not be put off with less than God himself," we all say, and still we hug our pet righteousness.

Jesus saw the man willing enough to be forgiven when his practice did him harm and the people condemned him, but holding on with unteachable devotedness while it pleased him and his neighbors praised him.

It lay along the line of doing as other rulers did and not being an independent king and nation setting a great example in David's time. So it must lie along some line where we as a nation want to do like other nations in our time. And it must lie along some line where as individuals we have been trying to maintain some standard set up by the community at large, or the world in general.

David never got an independent mind on one point, and all his surgical operations never stood him up independent of the examples of the other kings. And this lesson hints that neither as individuals nor as a nation, though we are on the eve of one sweet, new deliverance, is our final surgery accomplished with the great emancipation now about to take place.

Though the light is near, so near that the old kingdoms are tottering and personal events are making strong changes, still, we rigidly adhere for a while ahead, to the one usage whose every turn act as a blind against the meaning of the divine kindness with its sweet surgery.

According to this lesson we shall still stick to that rigidity held purpose of mind moving through every daily act of life which is the top root of our troubles, as personalities and as nations. These lessons have often come out straight in the matter, telling what is to cease in the lands. But they have spoken as prophecies of what should shortly be brought to pass. This lesson makes it clear that this present excitement is not the great and final campaign of independence for the people.

The Inter Ocean Newspaper, August 23, 1896

Lesson IX

Absalom's Defeat And Death

II Samuel 18:9-17

"Heartily know when half-gods go the gods arrive." Emerson

When a cheap friend plays you false, rejoice; his superior is about to appear. You are soon to have the genuine article. When a cheap constituency in whom you have had confidence, deserts you, rejoice; a noble body of appreciative mind is casting its comforting stature on the horizon.

The signals of futurity are many. Both transcendentalism and Bible announcements explicitly declare that it is silly to weep over any lost article, as its getting away with itself is sure evidence that something more satisfactory is near at hand. This is true in particular life; it is true in national life; it is true for the world.

These Bible lessons are calculated to show how history always is repeating itself. The sharp surgery by which Absalom was cut off from David caused Solomon to loom on the horizon of Israel as its coming King, with far more substantial greatness than Absalom had ever shown any signs of.

It is true that if David had adjusted his home life to the divine friend's influence he would not have been so brutally hurt by the necessary surgery. It is just as true in our particular cases that if we had known what operations to desist from the sharp trials of yesterday or today would never have had to take place. It is also true that if this Nation and all nations together had known what they were doing that was from first to last at variance with the divine order they might have spared themselves some of their severe experiences.

Inasmuch as it was divine surgery in answer to David's prayer, the outcome of it was excellent, for Solomon took Absalom's place as Crown Prince of Israel when that ambitious youth accidently disposed of himself in his efforts to dispose of David. (II Sam. 18:9-17) Applied to this age and Nation, it tells plainly that the present attempt to overthrow the people's rights will seem for a while to have all the advantages on its side, but by some sudden seeming accident it will go all to pieces.

Applied to individuals the experience will be the same. Some will have it sharp and hard, some light and easy, but all, together, the same experience simultaneously.

And both to national life and to individual life a new advantage will loom into sight, of which Solomon, 1023 B.C., was the prototype.

In the Bible it tells plainly what the stumbling block of iniquity is in our age, but it is mostly left for inference as to what was David's stumbling block.

Isaiah is full of descriptions of this age and time in his book of prophecies. In chapter 7, verse 19 he speaks of the final rising up of the people to cast off the usage sanctioned by the world now: "They shall cast the silver in the streets, and their gold shall be removed; their silver and their gold are the stumbling block of their iniquity." David's fornications, sanctioned by the world, were his stumbling block. The usage of gold and silver is the stumbling block of the Christian age, though sanctioned by the world. This reads as an improbable statement, but it is the truth.

And as David's pains came along the line of his home life as his darling son played him false, so the pains of the people of this age do all come along the silver and the gold line, as these two metals are played falsely with by being slid into the hands of the few leaving the many to scream in company with David; "Oh, my son, Absalom!" Verse 33 of the same 18th chapter.

With all the Bible information as to what gods in our age are hiding from man's life the true God, there is no mistaking where the world now stands. Solomon, Absalom, David career on the pages of antiquity to make it easy to see how things always come out. The prophecies are propositions, but the careers of men are demonstrations.

It is easy to explain that Absalom's name by signifying peace, which the Bible concordance always declare it does, must, perforce, bring David and his land a certain kind of peace, even if at the cost of a few human beings. It is easy to explain that by Absalom's riding on a mule he was stubbornly bent upon getting his own triumphs, peace or no peace. It is easy to say that since his unconscious purpose in life was to make a sort of peace, his stubbornness must stay him, because whatever a man's name means he is bound to exhibit, nolens volens. But such interpretations of scripture passages are not the deeper intentions of inspiration. They please the intellect and thousands of intellectually metaphysical people are now engaged in picking them to pieces after such mind-pleasing fashions. They really, however, are smothering to the breath of anybody who has breathed in wider skies of meaning.

It is a wider sky of meaning to appreciate that there is nothing new under the sun and that the instant we pick up a book with any story of a living career it is positively certain the beaming influence of divinity is bearing that story into our hands to tell us by pictures as well as by statements of enormous principles that we ourselves are now acting out in extra measure the movements of that story. For then we can see how we are coming out, we can see what to change, we can see how nations and individuals are dealing with each other, and how they are dealing with us personally. This may not strike the average reader as a fact at first, but as it is true, it is its own appeal. It soon shows its self evidence.

There is such a life possible as holding on to no ideas of mind which contradict the beaming influence of divinity shining now on us. That life of mind, it is declared, was really lived by one Jesus of Nazareth. There is such a life possible as holding on to no physical habit which contradicts the beaming influence of the divinity now shining on us. That life of the body, it is declared, was really lived by that same Jesus of Nazareth. For the scriptures say that he was tempted in all points, like us, yet was without any sin. That is, without a single clutch or any kind of thought, and without a single clutch on any bodily habit. Some men do not believe that Jesus of Nazareth lived without clutching at ideas and holding them like other men. They do not believe that he lived without clutching at bodily practices exactly like other men. In other words, they do not believe that an emancipated mind ever lived among men. They do not believe that an emancipated body ever walked on earth.

David of Israel three thousand years ago was the forerunner of Jesus very remarkably in that he was emancipated on all lines but one. Jesus coming after him was wholly emancipated. As long as we stick to anything so vitally essential to our happiness or comfort we are not emancipated in mind or body, and so we hold an imaginary Jesus

Christ before our own faces. We hold an imaginary Jehovah before our faces. Now an imaginary Jesus Christ is a poor stick. So is an imaginary Jehovah, or Lord, or God.

There is some evidence in this chapter that David believed in the doctrine of fate for he ran away from Jerusalem weeping and tearing his hair like an idiot when Absalom gathered a large force of men against him. But he believed it on the dark side, for he thought all the advantages belonged to those that hated him and all the disadvantages belonged to himself. He believed in the hand of God against him. His flight from Jerusalem was a coup de ma.itte, or master stroke in harmony with the surgical operation then divinely going on, but he wailed and screeched as though it were all disaster to himself. He never got over wailing at surgical operations during all the rest of his life. He ought to have had for his constant address to the beaming divinity that was shining on his life those wonderful words of the Brahmans: "I take my refuge in thy order, Ohm," for there is a sure refuge from personal calamity in Ohm. And Ohm never lets anybody make a false move of body or mind who has let go his last clutch. Ohm never lets any move of mind or body get us into actual trouble, even if we are clutching, but we shall have many outward signs or symptoms of trouble all the way of our clutching life.

The plain unvarnished title of this lesson is "Unclutch!" It is the first commandment put into a picture. It is the first commandment put into one word. The committee call the title "Absalom's Defeat and Death." Many clergyman are pointing warning fingers at Bryan as riding on a mule to his death. Some are pointing the same warning to McKinley, as riding on a mule to his death. But only one of them is really riding the mule into the woods of Ephraim in this campaign.

If in any way we are trying to undermine anybody, or in any way anybody is trying to undermine us, we are certainly at this moment riding our mule toward defeat. The beaming influence of the divinity now shining on us asks that we see its kindly strength, its kindly competency to handle our life even if we have no common sense of our own, no money, no friends, no army of any sort helping us. The less we have of these things the more of God we have. The more naked we are the more we feel the circumambient atmospheres. The more naked is our soul of the thoughts of mind which this world thinks, the clearer its appearance is like unto the all-soul.

Jesus saw that certain positive ideas were the governing potency of this world on the external plane. They are held tenaciously by all men in common. They cause their bodies to operate in certain ways, their tongues to speak in certain ways, their eyes to roll in certain ways. In none of these ways did he feel bound to think or act. He said: "The Prince of this world cometh and findeth nothing (like himself) in me." He was the detached one, the emancipated one. He was clearly the likeness of the all-soul.

Even after David, while watching the divine friend, had seen how skillful was his hand, he still wept and wailed. In prophecy we are told that when the silver and the gold of this world are suddenly made nothing as mediums of exchange, even though the people know that they have been the stumbling blocks of their iniquity, they shall weep and wail at their being demonetized. (Rev. 18) And we, even when we see that our disadvantages are removed, shall wail over them as though they were good things, gotten away from us.

We are told by this lesson that when the half gods go the gods arrive. So, let whatsoever we have prized be taken away from us, let us not wail as though something valuable had been removed, for this is the sign of our blurred eyesight, but rather let us rejoice that the incoming treasure is so wonderfully much better. If we cannot easily do this, how plain it is that we are among the clutchers.

There is no rapture in any experience that goes along with clutching. It is always so alloyed with apprehension that the pain is greater than the joy. The only rapture is in owning nothing, not even a good name, a grand throne. The sweetest life is the life so far out of the reach of the governing ideas of the apparent world that no good fame can help us and no bad fame can hurt us. David and Absalom are marked illustrations of the pangs of closing the teeth down on possessions such as are prized by the apparent world.

The constant allusion of the Bible waiters to an intelligent Friend moving is will upon the affairs of men gives the readers thereof a constant call to notice an unseen world in the midst of the seen. This is what makes it so inspiring to read the Bible. If one reads the Bible with notions of God in his mind such as other man and woman have given him, he is certain to think God is some very uncertain person giving his favors to a selected crew upon this earth and withholding all favors from the rest. But if one reads the Bible without holding on to any notions he soon finds that God is a mighty influence streaming through the universe, knowing nothing whatever of the affairs of men, but yet affecting all affairs, joyously when not opposing the influence, painfully when crossing it. And as we read on, we discover that the things that cross the beaming radiance are the last ones we are supposing. We discover that it is a very good thing to let go whatever crosses the shining path of the Almighty. It is a very good thing to offer it by name to the melting countenance of the only dissolver of the stumbling blocks.

There is nothing new under the sun. Not a religion is new, not a witticism is new. Not a historic transaction is new. Each one is a ball rolling itself over and over in space, and always going through the same gyrations over and over. Cervantes borrowed from the Greeks, the Greeks had borrowed the same from the Egyptians. Edgeworth borrowed from the Irish, the Irish had stolen the same from some people living 250 years before the New Testament. In Wendell Phillips' lecture upon the lost arts we are struck with astonishment to find that nothing new ever arrives upon our planet. So, these stories of the Bible tell what happened in all ages whensoever the same motive prompts the heart and stirs the body.

So these stories shall live as long as time unrolls her scrolls for man to print his repetitions of the past upon. And while the mind is still hugging its primitive delusions, and the body is still rolling its eyeballs, and fingering ledgers to catch happiness out of what crosses the divine influence, this story of David and Absalom shall gleam on the delusion-shadowed life to offer the way of surgery without pain.

Arise, as a strong God from his slumber, it is only God who is not clutching at something. God is too wise to hamper himself with wives and children and money and mules. The wiser a man is the less he owns. And the less he owns the more he is like himself. And at the point where he is himself he is the emancipated one.

Should it so be that at this moment any man should own nothing at all and thus be himself at his emancipation center, his influence would be God among us and to cross him would be to cross the Almighty.

Inter-Ocean Newspaper, August 30, 1896

Lesson X

The Crown Of Effort

I Chronicles 22:6-16

"Whatever obstacles control,
Thine hour will come; go on, true soul,
Thou'lt win the prize, thou'lt reach the goal."

With this lesson the triumph of the king is in sight. He is 70 years old, the time has been a long strain, the life journey has been rough, but the sweet end is close. (I Chron. 22:6-16) Everyone who had tried to thwart or spoil him is lost track of. He sits securely in his own throne, lord over his own environments, though not altogether conscious of all his rights.

Though this scripture selection made by the august board is great, applicable to each nation on earth and to the United States in particular, (as being the key-nation among them all), still it has such specially comforting intentions for each special reader that it is better to make it individual this time and let each individual apply it to the nation's career. It refers to the crown of effort. It refers to individual success.

There is such a thing as being good and doing right constantly and yet being constantly misunderstood and perpetually thwarted. This lesson refers to that feeling which stirs more or less in everybody, that if they had had a better chance, somehow, they would have been happier and come out more satisfactorily. It tells what that feeling signifies.

The lesson opens with the statement: "Then he called for Solomon." It was David who palled, without really realizing it. David had the key to the divine storehouse of love, wisdom, prosperity, health, life, peace, joy. The Bible is explicit about David's having the key to the divine storehouse. Isaiah tells of it in his twenty-second chapter. The author of the book of Job alludes to it in his twelfth chapter. St John speaks about it in his third Revelations.

For years nobody knew what that key of David could possibly be. The name of the Lord was in his heart, and as nearly as he could speak it aloud he had it on his lips also. He never told anybody what that name was, but that name was the key without doubt. It was the "open sesame" to whatever he wanted. By simply recognizing its presence in himself He felt its authority.

He felt the streaming warmth of the Divine One whose name he believed in. Under the glow and glory of that divine warmth he accomplished wonderful things. It was a wonderful thing to have given birth to so majestic and intelligent a child as Solomon. It was a wonderful thing to have all the invisible forces of the universe on his side through the irresistible goodness of the streaming warmth forever inspiring the atmosphere around him. It lighted his eyes with kingly fire, it pointed his tongue with eloquent charm, it quickened his brain with shining inventions.

All the strength of Omnipotence was back of David. Strange that he should have crossed it even on one line. But by crossing it on one line he had as rough a time of it as could be well imagined. Out of each turmoil he emerged conqueror, but by the time he was fifty years old he was calling for peace, peace, peace! His Bathsheba experiment was his most willful cross against the streaming warmth, so his greatest struggles were along that business. Therefore, his most triumphant emergence out of misery was the son of Bathsheba, who answered his prayers for peace, rich peace.

For Solomon was the oldest son of David's marriage with Bathsheba. And no king was ever richer than Solomon, no King's reign was ever more peaceable, no King ever rode in such glorious state, no King ever had so great a worldly learning, and no King ever set out upon his reign with so good a hold upon the eternally present God.

What David called for by name he got. As he called for rich peace he got it. In all probability he could have had the rich peace in his own life and mind if he had found out about how strong in the calling authority he was and how perpetually at right angles he was striking the eternal influence shining on his body. His actual answer stood before him in the noble person of Solomon, but not as he could have most wished.

These lessons are all mystic. Therefore they deal with the secret causes of things and events. They tell how the personal character of a monarch moves through the mental auras surrounding his people's heads. It is the same with Presidents and Czars as with Kings. If there is one particular trick in his character there will be a good deal of anarchism during the course of his dictatorship, or a good deal of poverty and panic.

The personal character of a sovereign subtly determines more than is generally believed. The Bible teaches this. The Bible tells of another mystic power. It is that of calling home to ourselves some of our widely dispersed knowledge. It tells plainly that everything we can ever have any dealing with starts first from our own central place. It is spread abroad, and we see, hear, feel, or see it as though somebody else or some other power had manufactured it. Sometimes we spread it afar so widely that we do not see it all. Calling; and calling, and calling it, will bring it into sight. So this Bible lesson opens with its secret, sacred, personal instruction to each of us to call for what we want. Call and get it. "Call and I will answer thee." "And it shall come to pass that before they call I will answer." "Call thou upon me in the day of adversity."

The things we imagine are the things we have once set going. If we want them again we must call them back to us. Forms are callable. Have not many people seen again their friends whom they thought dead, by calling, and calling, and calling their names? Have not powers been restored by calling them to return? Eyesight has come back again which by some unwilling and unconscious action people had sent away to some great distance from them. Hearing has come back, to its proper home in some people's ears. So has happy health. Nothing can get too far away to be called back again.

Thus when David called for peace and still did the things that acted against his peace, of course he had Solomon, the embodiment of peace, come close to him for his heart to rejoice in. The ability to call and get is the mark of authority set in the foreheads of the cheapest and meanest people equally strongly with the richest and wisest ones. The key of David lay in the fact that he used the authority he felt from the name he spoke. Let the car driver who thinks he has been defrauded of something by somebody, simply know that whatever is gone out of sight is still within calling distance. He need not call so that the riders in his cars can hear his voice, but with his silent energy let him call back his lost possession from over the hills and seas.

Let the ignoramus whose intelligence has spread itself afar from himself call back his own intelligence to its nest in his head.

"David called for Solomon his son." Wisdom is the son or daughter of everybody. In David's case it was "he". In Mordecai's case it was "she". In Solomon's case it was "it".

There are many illustrations of people's having called for their vanished powers, and they have come trooping back.

This set of good and kind people now living on this earth to whom everything has been disappointments, with whom everybody was always finding fault, let them call for the kindness they have spread out so far, dispersed so widely, to come back to them again.

And its waters returning back to their fountain, shall fill them full of refreshment.

Some people are always giving good messages to others, but getting complaints and bad news to themselves all the time. Two such people, catching hold of David's key, called for good news, and kept palling till they were overwhelmed with the good news that began pouring in to them. This is the practice of the presence of good.

All Christian science is reasoned out by the statements of the presence of the good in this universe, as waiting everywhere to be seen plainly by being named and acknowledged. But this David tells us plainly that the good he was after was first sent forth from himself, and then called back to himself when he got ready.

This David tells us plainly by this chapter exactly what Jesus told more than a thousand years afterward, that is, "I said ye are gods." David sang it with timbrels and harps. Jesus spake it in wonderful tones. The God authority vested in all men alike, whereby their lost powers, their vanished beauties, their departed joys, their escaped health, may come bounding, rushing, running swiftly back to their home nest, whence they first hailed from.

"By this knowledge that ye are the king, from whose central place all things first sprang forth, and now exist somewhere, do you henceforth be wholly prospered," said David to Solomon in verse 11. Then David showed Solomon quantities of silver and gold that he had called unto himself easily while he was in turmoil on other lines, and had never found out even at 70 years of age what he had been in so much trouble for. He insisted that he was a great sinner in some mysterious way, but in what way was past his count. He had much forgiveness. That is, for his pains he had much peace. For his troubles he had much joy. But one particular joy, the joy of being the owner of all of himself, he never had.

He never called home to himself the dispread satisfaction in being himself as he was, one in substance with the very God whom he praised.

But he told Solomon to exercise the authority that was in him to do the things he himself had not done. He had grown tired with wondering what he was doing that was so unlike his friend's wishes that he was now calling for a grave to rest in. So he crawled into a grave to rest shortly after the conversation recorded in this lesson.

But as rest is something that can come without crawling into a grave, this lesson urges all men to get rest by the exercise of their authority to call rest home again to themselves wherever they have shed it afar off as David had. For David said that there should be no rest while he was King. (Verse 8 and 9) He saw Solomon not having any actual rest either; for many years ahead, "Arise, and be doing my son." (Verse 16)

This section gives the whole solution of the prayer scheme of the saints of earth in all ages. They have taken a very roundabout way of drawing their own possessions home to themselves, but during their hours of agonizing appeals they have called enough times and with energy enough so that the possessions have come sailing and riding along in due season. And this they have always called answer to prayer.

When any man knows the authority vested within himself to call his own strayed greatness back again, he stands exactly with Jesus on the upland spot remembering his own native glory saying: "Glorify thou me with the glory that I had with thee before the world was."

It is time this Nation remembered her own splendid independence, which she had been so generously yielding up, and gathered it again to herself. It is time that each man, each woman, each child, on this planet, should be told how by some unwilling unconscious process they have spread far off their wisdom, their strength, their beauty, their sweetness, their consciousness of their own identification with authority, and how by drawing it again to themselves they may again be in full sight of the world, the same great characters they were at the daybreak, while the morning stars were singing and the oceans of eternity were hymning their true all-conquering names.

The day breaks again on the borders of time, and the shadows flee away. The cross we have set against the beaming light comes down. The rest we know we have given so far away we call it again. The joy in the possession of our restored self as it was in the beginning we call home again. The prosperity we have let others have as far as the mind could stretch, we draw it hither again. The name of the Lord which we have scattered abroad we gather it in again.

The lost word we catch in its might again. David taught us by dropping his key and so often forgetting his own oneness with his divine comrade as much as by his daily remembrance of that comrade's omnipotence. Taking note by him we will not forget but forever remember that at our central place we are authority one and the same as the Father. Whatever we ask for is ours by virtue of having once sent it forth from ourselves. The everlasting text of divine dominion is, "David called for Solomon."

Inter-Ocean Newspaper, September 6, 1896

Lesson XI

"Thy Gentleness Hath Made Me Great"

II Samuel 22

> All my emprises have been filled with thee;
> My speculations, plans, begun and carried on in thoughts of thee.
> Sailing the deep or journeying the land for thee;
> Intentions, purports, aspirations mind, leaving results to thee.
> O, I am sure they really came from thee,
> The urge, the ardor, the unconquering will,
> The potent, felt, interior command, stronger than words,
> A message from the heavens whispering to me even in sleep,
> These sped me on.
> — "Columbus," by Walt Whitman

The chapter for today's consideration is II Samuel, 22. The secret influence of the chapter comes from the last clause of the thirty-sixth verse, viz.: "Thy gentleness hath made me great." And again the lesson applies so wonderfully to the individual, that, though it is meant to rouse the national courage, it must be taken personally, individually. For see, it tells what is going on while ever there seems least going on in behalf of anybody and everybody who is today doing the very best he can, with his hopes centered on the fact of a living, present, active God, standing by his right hand.

How gentle would the Almighty One have to be in order to equate him to almighty gentleness? Surely he would have to be almighty still. Supremely active in supreme inactivity. And thus it is that the wonderful God has always inspired those who knew him best to say, "My ways are not your ways; neither are my thoughts your thoughts." For, while men do what they do by scrambling and hustling, noise and motion, the wonderful God does everything by gentleness so sweet that it seems to everybody as if nothing at all were being done.

And this is the text of the lesson: "Thy gentleness hath made me great." And this is the influence of the text: Courageous certainty that everything is this minute working just as it ought to work in our own particular behalf. Nothing that is happening can help us; nothing can hinder us. The trend of events is our joyous release from all that binds us down. Everything that seems against us is really for us. Everything that seems for us is no more for us than what seems against us. The Lord omnipotent is our changeless friend in storm and calm alike. He is our rock, our fortress, our deliverer.

To get this courageous confidence men have starved and beaten their bodies, they have punished their children's bodies, they have prayed night and day. It has been the quest of men in all ages. It is your quest, my reader. How greatly above your surroundings you become the instant one waft of courageous confidence from the uplands of God blows aside the fear in your heart. Read again the secreatest text of this day's lesson. Lift up your eyes to the ever- bending tenderness now watching you. "Thy gentleness hath made me great."

The offer of Jesus Christ to man was greatness. Such greatness that at the presentation of death man should be able to say: "I am master over you." Such greatness that at the presentation of disease to man he should be able to say: "I am master over, you." Such greatness that when the fires and floods and lions' jaws should open their mouths at him, and no arm should be nigh to save him, no eye to pity him, he could rise up in smiling indifference, knowing, "I am master over you." Such greatness that all the ignorance of an earth of born and unborn multitudes not knowing even the name of their mighty Savior, being presented to him, with no instructor nigh, and no kindness anywhere to see, he should rise up with all the knowledge of which all men are capable and declare that he had letters though he had never learned.

At every turn he should be greater, consciously greater, than any obstacle that could be presented to him. Today's lesson rings like a golden hammer on harp strings of sacred steel the ravishing refrain of David; "Thy gentleness hath made me great."

Forever the omnipotent One seemed to be doing nothing for Jesus. Yet on that arm relying he knew that Pilate's mob was powerless to hurt him. On that face ever gazing he lifted up his voice and wept that the sound of his sobs on the air of eternity might teach how tender is the heart of man, though all men have the name of being cruel. He stretched out the arms of helplessness, touching the helpless arms of countless born and unborn men that he, feeling the thrilling strength behind him of the everlasting "I Am", might pass the strength of God from arm to arm the whole earth round. Yet, at this very point of his divinest greatness the do-nothing gentleness of Jehovah-Jireh (Signifies the I AM provider) was so much his that the commonest soldiers of Rome's brutal army spat into his face.

Today's lesson speaks of David, ancestor of Jesus, on both the father and the mother's side. This David had been many times sorely beset by seeming enemies, but no matter how formidable the enemies were, he was always conqueror over them.

It is well known to all the regular readers of these lessons that David of ancient Jewry was prototype of the government of a people by the people for the people. For David was a man of the people.

And as David suffered through constantly falling in with an international usage, and never standing up in the strength of his independent inspiration, all governments of a people, by the people, for the people, must suffer for falling in with an international usage, which is opposition to the divine inspirations that are forever streaming down, teaching to stand up in the independence of original action.

The lesson of August 30 told plainly what David's cross was made of, and also told what the cross of the last days of the materially minded world is to be made of. According to prophecy that cross of David had to come down, and according to prophecy that cross of this people has to come down. According to Jesus, when any house gets divided against itself its end is near. And now that silver money and gold money have got to fighting each other, each enlisting strong men and able women on its side, the end must be somewhere near.

But if the emprises of a single man, his speculations, plans, have all been lodged in God, and the emprises, speculations, plans of countless men of this Nation have been so lodged, then the falling of the house of the world, built of silver and of gold, shall not shake him or them or the Nation. And, whether one man ascends the chair of administration or another man wins it, shall not, cannot, count even a straw's weight against the great fall and the great exposure. "For we know that if our earthly house of this tabernacle be dissolved, we have a building of God, a house not made with hands."

That which is on the way, borne on the winds of resistless purpose, influence, divine breath, is coming into plain exposure, plain sight, and none can stop it. So all enthusiasm for one metal may as well be laid aside as enthusiasm for another. The winds of prophesy are blowing. The bugle tones of time's last anthems are in the Nations' ears. Salute no man with his bag of theories tied round his neck, by the way of thy glad march on the plateaus of the confidence, that this secret golden text inspires: "Thy gentleness — yes, gentleness, which has seemed to leave us flat, stale, and unprofitable — hath made us great." And none can hedge or hide or mar our great mastery over the presented terrors of the hour.

That which is true of our personal mastery now, over our personal obstacles, is true of our Nation also. The impossible is that which shall be accomplished. Note this grand choral of the Davidson choir, instigated by David himself, with the necks of all earthly obstacles under his feet:

"Thou hast given me the necks of my enemies. Then did I beat them small as the dust. Thou hast kept me to be the head of the heathen. Strangers shall submit themselves to me. Strangers shall fade away. The Lord liveth, and blessed be my rock, and exalted be the God of the rock of my salvation." — (Verses 41-47)

Enemies are obstacles, floods, famines, swords, sorrowful hearts, ignorance, death. The God of ages himself is above all else the greatest enemy, obstacle.

"Behold, I am against thee," saith the Lord. The Lord God omnipotent is to be laid hold of and used as a man would use a sword or pruning hook or painter's brush. He that drafteth the Almighty into his service is as powerful as the Almighty. Hear the talk of all the pulpits through ages on ages. Note how they have felt the opposition of the great and mighty "I Am".

How they have accused him of laying yokes on human necks and miseries on human lives. And how they have deplored his awful stillness — his masterly inactivity — not knowing that in that masterly inactivity was his absolute gentleness his lamb-like, fightless innocence, his docile friendship, capable of beating ignorance small as the dust of the earth; capable of setting hitherto undiscovered substances at our disposal; capable of dissolving the mountain peaks of human high and valley ways of human low into naught by the plain exposure of the glorious soul forever present in all men alike.

Lo! keen-eyed science,

> As from tall peaks the modern overlooking,
> Successive flats issuing.
> Yet, again, lo! the soul above all science.

Men have put different interpretations upon these verses where David's choir sang for him his words:

> Thou hast given me the necks of my enemies.
> Then did I beat them small as the dust.
> Strangers shall submit themselves to me.
> Strangers shall fade away.

Some say that enemies and strangers are evil thoughts. But away beyond thoughts run the splendors of that God whose gentleness makes me so great, and thee so great, and America so great, and Japan so great, and Corea (Korea) so great, and Patagonia so great, through some single heart within us, man, woman, or nation, lodging all his emprises in the gentle, inactive, all-powerful God.

Famine, fear, ignorance, are the enemies of a nation. See America put their necks under her feet because of somebody within her borders, nay many people together putting all their ventures on the back of the docile God.

See all who are doing this making nothing, nothing at all, of the obstacles called great by those who feel that they must scramble round and grind and rush to accomplish the tasks of this hour. "Is anything too hard for me?" saith the Lord. No. David's answer 1,000 years before our era is answer now: "With thee girding me I beat them small as the dust of the earth."

It is necessary for those to whom the great inventions and untold substances of earth are strangers to find the mighty One who can expose them, so that David's triumphant chorus may be theirs also. "Strangers submitted unto me. Strangers faded away." This wonderful One, to whom have been laid all the obstacles of human life, and in whose power are all the dissolvings of obstacles, can show the cheapest tramps among us how to make gold, how to make silver, how to have wisdom, how to discover all mysteries.

There are slight signals on the skies of this age to indicate how strangers shall submit right soon to man's demand for help. Has not Dr. Emmans, the inventor of an explosive, discovered how to make four ounces of gold out of six ounces of silver by the use of some intense energy which changes the molecular structure of the silver? How cheaply or how dearly will gold be held when it is found that all the rich silver mines are really gold mines in disguise.

How rich will it make the Rothschilds, who are buying American silver at 67 cents per ounce, to loan to China, to pay off her indemnity to Japan with? The instant this silver can all be converted into gold, what value will be set on gold? Who can tell? How that so-called mountainous difference between these two metals will fade away under the breath of the once stranger process. The gentle God is not inadequate on any line.

"Ye shall defile also the images of silver and the images of gold. Thou shalt say unto it go hence."

The lesson of today points to the accomplishment of the hitherto impossible, both for nations and for men. It touches the hinges of the gates leading to the last era of submission to earthly man and earthly conditions.

It comes swinging its glad requiems to the burdening past and its triumphant anthems to the unburdened future. As plainly as a voice can tune its heavenly chords it stands out on the pages of our Bible as written words and through the silent midnights of hoary time it sings into the hearts of every reader strange influences that he or she may feel, this instant, the touch of the gentle, all-competent God.

Softer than the south wind on the cheek of an infant is the touch of the Messiah on the heart of man today. But in its supernal gentleness is its supernal ability.

What though you and I be cheap and defeated and ignorant and useless, the less we are the nearer the gentle One we are. And the less we claim to do the more we leave for him, the docile God, to work out in his own wondrous way. The heathen forces, the elements of nature, now yield for our sake to his way.

Soar and rush, great world, he that accomplisheth great things is still. Scream and orate, ye noisy crew, he that shaketh the earth whispereth so low that the stars of the deep nights of Sahara have to stop their soundless wheels on the ethers of the sleeping, solemn skies to catch his meaning: "Thy gentleness, O God, maketh me great."

Inter-Ocean Newspaper, September 13, 1896

Lesson XII

A Fool For Christ's Sake

Proverbs 16:7-33

That "unconquerable will" which Columbus felt within himself was the divine influence pushing his particular life to a fruition.

Everybody is gifted with something unconquerable. It pushes itself out to fruition in and through him early or late. If one does now and then seem to have accomplished nothing at all it simply means that he belongs to some other realm, some different clime toward which his unfitted feet are hurrying.

Today's Bible lesson calls all people who amount to nothing on this earth by the general title of "fools." In the Hebrew there are said to be several words which can be translated into English as fool. One is the evil-minded man who is in the scripture called a fool. One fool is the self-confident person who never listens to other people's propositions, but carries out his own, no matter who is disadvantaged. One is the fool with no ideas. Learned commentators of the Bible texts say that the fool alluded to in this lesson is the evil-minded person. (Proverbs 16:22-13)

If any of us are arranging to live and think as though the divine presence in the universe were an actual one, we shall have some one very marked and prominent event in our experience every week, corresponding always to the theme of the international lessons. If we are mostly engaged on other lines and mostly doubtful about the practicability of the divine one's interest in our welfare, we shall have each experience belonging to the lesson in a minor way. It will come in as a side event.

Last week's lesson showed this point very clearly. It taught that whoever was having great difficulties to overcome would see them melt into thin air by the influence of the great God who seemed to be doing nothing at all. It was a lesson to which the world might pin its faith and rest content. It ought to be the golden text of every day in the year while time doth last. It is the actual keynote to the life of Jesus. How, if anybody has been watching the heavenly presence steadfastly he has already proved the text of last week's lesson.

This lesson is its twin. It tells how like fools we appear if we are leaning heavily on the arm of the omnipotent upbearing breath of the heavens and earth. To some we appear empty-headed, to some we appear to be self-confident and inconsiderate, to some we appear to be evil-minded. Yet, truly, we are none of these, but only unfitted feet traveling unknown paths toward the wonderful sun where our life will be good for something.

Columbus being jeered at by the boys and nobles of Spain was a pretentious fool to them. Yet his restless feet were hurrying him over still more restless waters to unknown America. He is as good an example as any of the way the world has always looked upon unfitted feet. Julius Caesar was rather a good example. He had epileptic fits and seemed to be as feeble in wits as in backbone.

"It doth amaze me that a man of such a feeble temper should so got the start of this majestic world and bear the palms alone. Upon what meat hath this our Caesar fed that he is grown so great?"

All tramps and criminals are only unfitted feet, hurrying restlessly toward their sunlit native land, where the glory of their here-chilled genius may blazon forth. John the Revelator says that in the days when we are wisely watching the divine One with the expectation of help on our daily path we shall not have to wait to get into our rightful country by the gates of death, but shall all rise into the beautiful exhibition of our genius here on this earth. See Rev. 11. The mission therefore, of this lesson is to undo the bars of death.

Something occurs to people who keep their hopes and hearts fixed on the wonderful God. They do not act the same as their neighbors. They do nothing where their neighbors would spread and bluster. They say nothing when to speak would give them luster. This lesson says that their advices are ridiculous, their attempts all seem wicked or forward (perverse) or violent. Nobody likes them and they are the failures of human society, to all appearances. But the lesson closes by declaring that their lot was cast into their lap exactly like other men's lots, and that their whole handling of life is by their Lord, exactly like other men. (Verse 33) "The lot is cast into the lap, but the whole disposition thereof is of the Lord."

"Lord" is the principal idea we hold. No matter what our lot is, we govern it by our principal idea. Some people have great wealth, but have an idea they are poor. They govern themselves to look and act like poor people. We all know persons with this "Lord". Some people have great talents in plain sight of their neighbors, but they do not believe these talents are worth anything, and so they never shine out as talented. Their "Lord" does not let them. Some people have disadvantages at every turn, but they have an idea that by extra effort they can beat their way through hard luck and amount to something. Their "Lord" leads them a tremendous chase.

The lot cast into our lap is the subject of this lesson, together with the disposition of it by our "Lord". The "lot" is the secret influence of the still, moveless God. The "Lord" is the controlling idea.

The controlling idea is sometimes kind, sometimes satanic. Columbus had a controlling idea which he caught from the lot cast into his lap. This was lucky for him in his generation. The "fool" feels the presence of his lot, but his main idea interferes with it. He cannot make his feeling and his idea match. If his "Lord" or controlling idea suits the world he is praised. If his controlling idea does not suit the world he is called evil-minded, empty-headed or pretentious.

This lesson calls upon us to see that all so-called evil-minded people and stupid are those who happen to have a "Lord" we do not like. But this lesson says they are moved into paths we dislike by not being able to make their lot serve them as they would like. It makes them restless.

The teachings of Jesus Christ were meant to show every man how to watch the lot cast into his lap, and catch his cue, or Lording idea, from that, instead of from his neighbors.

Jesus had a lot cast into his lap no better than any other man's. The Giver of lots is an impartial Being. Then Jesus watched his lot as his fine gold theme-thread, or shining substance, exactly like the One who gave it. He watched it until he saw that his lot was not money, not friendship, not honors, not family and farms. He saw that it was the all-conquering, all-owning Me. This roused his ideas all together to be united with the lot — the all-competent Me. Thence-forward he spent all his time showing how to change men's "Lord." "And as many as received him, to them gave he power to become the sons of God."

This text means that all who listened to his words felt his influence and took hold of their original lots with accurate ideas. "Sons of God," are accurate ideas of how to deal with our lot. The disappearance of this present lord, the coming of the Lord who is Lord indeed, is urged in this lesson.

To this day there is nothing that alters the way we handle our lot, casting out our old, driving "Lord," equal to the reception of the same power he gave. He knew his own Me. Then he knew that everybody who would know him would know their own me. The real lot is of the Me of each one of us. The Lord that disposes of that lot is our ruling idea.

Jesus Christ, even as a name repeated over and over, is to this day capable of changing our ruling idea. Nothing else and no other power can possibly save us from our present governing idea, whether it be one that suits our neighbors or not. The nearer a man comes to having insight enough to measure his own possibilities and put them out, the nearer he touches his divine lot; but nobody has really touched his Me, or lot, while ever he has the lording idea that he has to scramble, struggle, study, earn, learn, drive, wear, sweat, tire, or hire for the purpose of seeing his divine Me, his shining genius, his splendid lot, bloom out into some supernal achievement.

This is transcendentalism. Looking around we discover that nobody has ever proved any such wonderful proposition in its perfect measure. It does not follow; however, that nobody ever will prove it, simply on the ground that nobody ever has, for this lesson declares that nobody can prove it till they have the right "Lord."

Today's lesson strikes its soft radiance through our life, whatever it may seem to be, and as we watch its lovely meanings of the text we feel our old lord dissolving never to appear again. Even the lord that has pleased our neighbors is dissolving. How can we therefore please those neighbors any more with our former ways if those ways are gone? So that it amounts to one and the same thing so far as our foolishness is concerned, in the estimation of our neighbors, whether we have a positive lord they call us unpleasant names about, or drop the old lord they admired, as we let it dissolve in the Christ Jesus, meant by the silent voice of this selection from Proverbs. This is being fools for the divine sake. To the world's opinion we are as deadly silly as the lord they liked is dissolving in the melting smile of the divine lot when we find it.

The committee on Bible texts looks at them very differently from what the Transcendentalist or deep student of the Jesus Christ word does. That committee is governed to a man, by a "lord", which his neighbors all praise.

Not one of them has ever been a fool for Christ's sake, or any other sake? Not one of them ever was called "empty-headed."

Inter-Ocean Newspaper, September 20, 1896

LESSON XIII

The Lord Is A Strong Tower

REVIEW

Proverbs 28:10

This lesson shows the difference between Jacob's practice of the presence of Divinity and the practice carried on by Jesus. Jacob made a bargain with the presence; Jesus commanded it. Jacob said he would call Jehovah his God and set up a stone to his name if he would give him plenty to eat and lead him home to his father's house. Jesus said: "My kingdom come, thy will be done. Give us this day our daily bread."

The subject of the lesson is put forth by the religious conclave as "The Gain of Walking in God's Way." The subject of the lesson, as put forth by the golden text, is "There Is Neither Gain Nor Loss in Christ Jesus."

The golden text teaches over again one of the blessedest facts ever exposed in man, viz: Neither male nor female, neither high nor low, in Christ Jesus; neither learned nor unlearned, neither profit nor loss, neither black nor white, in Christ Jesus. It brings up again on the mystic pages of the indestructible Bible the secret of life and omnipotence, viz.: That all things in heaven above, earth beneath, and waters under the earth are responsively obedient to the spoken orders of man. The man may be a bootblack or a Czar in the realm of distinctions, but in the realms of dictation he is King and priest after the order of Melchizedek, and his rank, as rated there, is that all things are his and stand around exactly as he decrees.

In the realm of dictation every man, woman, and child sees clearly that a stone is a stone because he told it to be so; that slavery and pain prance over the planet because he told them to. In the realm of dictation man sees how pliable the whole universe is to his declarations. He sees how his eyes can command the mountains, how his voice can sway the cyclones, how his hand can rock the oceans. In the realm of dictation man detects that he has never lost anything, that he has never gained anything. He sees that all things are arranged or disarranged by himself, made painful or joyful by himself, raised up and set down by himself. In the realm of dictation man finds his kingship, which he had before ever he set the golden stars to singing or watched for the melting away of the skies.

In the realm of dictation, open to the tramp as freely as to the Kaiser, man sees himself no longer a sniveling suppliant before the throne of some invisible tyrant, begging for a chance to work for the oil trust at $1 a day. He sees himself no longer as a pitiful rag in the winds of nature. He knows better than to ask any favor of an invisible King on a throne. He does not whine before some unreliable power with a name which he is told is not really known to anybody and ask for health, wealth, or wisdom. In the realm of dictation man makes no Jacob bargains with the owners of the mines and pasture lands, to do so and so if the owner will do so and so. In this realm man finds out how much of the pasture lands and mines he himself owns, and always has owned, since before time set her dials to turning their styluses on the faces of people and trees.

This lesson declares that there is some name now offered among men which has an awakening power in it sufficient to stir up everybody who uses it, so that he can see and feel who he himself is. This name, it is said, can rouse up the sleeping kingship in the charwoman who sweeps cellars, so that she is able to see that her sweeping of cellars is her own self-elected performance through using her kingly power in that direction. This name shows her herself as she is, in all the glory she had once, which she owns now, and which she can never get rid of.

The power in this name is the waking sweetness of remembering what house we are in and what are our rights in this house. The power in this name is the waking joy of finding that the great caravan of earth is a picture conjured up by ourselves, to be let go of when we please.

The world has had a tricky lingo going on for ages that this awakening name is lost. The Bible tells plainly that it is not lost. The Bible tells in the old dispensation the names of men who used the awakening word. It tells in the new dispensation what name will bring it to remembrance. It says that it will not sound on the ears nor blow like a breath on the flesh. It will not be a sight to the eyes nor an object for the fingers to catch at. But, yet, whoever remembers it is king by the fiery beauty of his eyes, the irresistible sweetness of his voice, the magical joyousness of his touch. The universe obeys him. Not because he has some new power given him, but because he is aware of his old power.

Jacob called everything he seized hold of a gain. Jesus called everything he touched his own from eternity's opening point to eternity's close. If a man gains anything somebody is bound to lose something. This is Jacob's pious joy. If a man only takes his own, and all men own exactly alike, nobody gains and nobody loses by the man's taking. This is the practice of the majestic Jesus.

"Where I am there ye may be also."

"And Jacob vowed a vow, saying; 'If God will be with me and will keep me in the way that I go and will give me bread to eat and raiment to put on, so that I come again to my father's house in peace; then shall the Lord be my God, and this stone which I have set for a pillar shall be God's house, and of all that thou shalt give me I will surely give the tenth unto thee." (Gen 28:20) Thereupon Jacob proceeded to plunder from Laban and succeeded. (Gen. 30)

"And Jesus lifted up his eyes to heaven and said: 'Father the hour is come; glorify thy son that thy son also may glorify thee." (John 17:1) Thereupon Jesus began to call the world to rest in his omnipotent bosom.

The golden text reads: "The name of the Lord is a strong tower, the righteous runneth into it and is safe." (Proverbs 18:10)

It means that everybody who remembers the least bit of his own kingship does what he pleases and nothing can prevent him. If he feels a conscious glow of ability to do what he sets out to do he is remembering a little of his omnipotence. Jacob robbed Esau because he felt able to do it. He plundered from Laban because he felt able to do so. Whenever he lost the memory of his kingship he strengthened and pulled till he remembered it again. Jesus did not once forget his kingship. He offered his name as the name that would cause all the world to remember their native rights. "The

Holy Spirit whom the Father will send in my name shall teach you all things and call all things to your remembrance."

Every gold text used by the millions on millions of Protestant Sunday schools carries with it a potentiality belonging to itself. Subtly it steals into each heart and each life with its influence. There is a way of opening the mind to receive this Influence so that there is no strain of effort to get it, and yet the mind and life are wakened to a more natural state. There is such a thing as being able to detect the special influence of a golden text. The Influence of this text is, without doubt, to more or less awaken us to remembrance of our own executiveness as it used to be, as it is really in the present and as it always will be in the future.

The recollection of self is our greatest awakening. It is only partial awakening to bargain with the omnipotent force that swings the universe, promising that we will give our goods for a little attention from him, as Jacob did, and as the international title of the lesson reads.

This title implies that man gains something he did not before possess by keeping up a set of actions or a set of formulas prescribed by priests who had consumption of the lungs, weak eyesight, or lame legs. If those formulas and performances had not cured those priests how could other men hope to be cured by them? Therefore what gain could there possibly be in walking according to anybody's directions?

This golden text tells plainly that righteousness consists in waking up to understand our own rights. It tells that the word "Lord" as used in this way, refers to the dictating one whose everlasting headquarters are focused into our own self, no matter what may be our rank, whether rag-picker or Bishop. It tells of some name of this Me which can wake us to our dictating kingship as practiced by Jesus, and relieve us of our dickering habits as practiced by Jacob. It teaches that bargaining with the intelligent forces of the universe will be successful in a sense just as Jacob succeeded, but as dickering, trading, bargaining, arguing with anybody always puts us on rank with the one we talk to, so Jacob kept himself in the attitude of a trader as long as he lived, because he made a trader of the Almighty.

It tells that there is no need to command our fellow man, but to recollect his native kingship. It tells that nature is as obedient as a trained dog to the awakened one. It tells that there is certain waking up for anybody who catches the waking name. And this waking up sets the tongue to a new language, the eyes to a new vision, the hands to new tasks. This waking up is mortality putting on immortality. It is the immortal in man that is king over animals and nature. It is the immortal in man which is secure from both pain and pleasure. It is the immortal in man which never lays out a moral path for people to walk in, nor points out an immoral path as dangerous for them.

The immortal majesty in mankind would be immoral if it dickered with immorality, even to hate it. The immoral majesty would change its standards to suit the times by having eight or ten, or a hundred wives in Jacob's time, and one wife in Queen Victoria's time if it watched for immorality. It would make hanging right in one country and flogging for the same offense right in another country at one and the same instant if it had to dicker about right and wrong.

The Immortal Lord meant by this golden text is not so politic and tricky. "I am the Lord; I change not," saith he.

The Immortal Lord meant by this golden text is the changeless king preferring not to forget himself. Recollecting himself by the pronunciation of his own name he is his own safety. Recollecting his rights by the pronunciation of his own name he rejoices in being a strong tower more powerful than any assault of time or cyclone, or earthquake, either material or mental.

"The name of the Lord is a strong tower." (Proverbs 28:10)

"In my name cast out devils." (Mark 16:17)

"In my name speak with new tongues." (Mark 16:17)

"The Lord hear thee in the day of trouble. The name of the God of Jacob defend thee." (Psalm 20:1)

"Thy name is as ointment poured forth." (Songs of Solomon 1:3)

"For when two or three are gathered together in my name there am I in the midst of them. If two of you shall agree upon earth as touching any one thing that he shall ask it shall be done. (Matt. 18)

This awakening name is not a new name. "Thy name, O Lord, endureth forever." It is not a lost power which we recollect by using this name. "Lo, I am with you alway, even to the end of the world." We do not become some new characters when we use this name. "Before the day was, I am he." We are not changed from one substance to another by waking up and being natural. "Enter now into the joy of thy Lord." "Wake thou that sleepest."

This awakening name causes us to remember and remember till we were in the glory that we had before the world was.

In view of the fact that the mysterious Bible, which nobody can dispute and which is always getting the better of its opponents, is full of declarations about the rousing power in some name it is strange that more has not been said about what this name might be.

People trying to recollect where they came from before they suddenly discovered themselves walking as flesh and brain on this earth, have often declared that they have been here before, and are now here again; that is all. They declare that they have been here many times, going over and over again in the round of brain and flesh, this same earthly career. What makes them speak in this way? It is because they elect to remember in mortality. The rousing name of which the Bible speaks causes us to remember in immortality.

In this name there is no recollection of having been here before as flesh and brain wearing and worrying ourselves out with pain and pleasure, ignorance and learning. In this name there is one recollection only, that is the recollection of our authority as kings and priests after the order of Melchizedek. That is, ministers with self recollection judging the earth.

Those who do not recollect their own kingship carry the weight of the world on their heads and mourn over their own ignorance. Those who do not recollect their own kingship carry the weight of the world on their backs and mourn over the sufferings of all mankind. Those who do not recollect their own kingship carry the weight of the world in their arms and mourn over the sins of the people. Those who recollect their own kingship let the earth fall under their feet and walk over it in conscious dignity and grandeur.

This lesson is called "review" by the committee. Whoso reviews in mortality finds sins to sandpaper out of his neighbors. He finds sufferings to amputate from his neighbors. He finds ignorance to scrub out of their brains. But whoso recollects in the immortality wakened by the name mentioned in the Bible, rests from his labors and yet glorious works follow in his wake. He finds the deserts all abloom for his coming. He leaves the dry plains all green where his footsteps have been.

There are no dead where the sound of his voice beats the dusky stillness. The sick suddenly discover their everlasting health. The ignorant smile because they easily remember all the learning that scholars have been so sedulously seeking.

The poor find out their unchanged inheritance, Ah! The poor have the gospel preached in the smile of the face of him that recollects himself.

If ever there has walked one man on the earth with all things in it under his feet obedient unto him, why should we not listen to his directions if he gave any? Why not, indeed? "If a man keep my name he shall not see death." I am the resurrection and the recollection. My word shall not pass away.

Inter-Ocean Newspaper September 27, 1896

Notes

Other Books by Emma Curtis Hopkins

- *Class Lessons of 1888 (WiseWoman Press)*
- *Bible Interpretations (WiseWoman Press)*
- *Esoteric Philosophy in Spiritual Science (WiseWoman Press)*
- *Genesis Series 1894 (WiseWoman Press)*
- *High Mysticism (WiseWoman Press)*
- *Self Treatments with Radiant I Am (WiseWoman Press)*
- *The Gospel Series (WiseWoman Press)*
- *Judgment Series in Spiritual Science (WiseWoman Press)*
- *Drops of Gold (WiseWoman Press)*
- *Resume (WiseWoman Press)*
- *Scientific Christian Mental Practice (DeVorss)*

Books about Emma Curtis Hopkins and her teachings

- *Emma Curtis Hopkins, Forgotten Founder of New Thought – Gail Harley*
- *Unveiling Your Hidden Power: Emma Curtis Hopkins' Metaphysics for the 21st Century (also as a Workbook and as A Guide for Teachers) – Ruth L. Miller*
- *Power to Heal: Easy reading biography for all ages – Ruth Miller*

To find more of Emma's work, including some previously unpublished material, log on to:

www.highwatch.org

www.emmacurtishopkins.com

WISEWOMAN PRESS
Vancouver, WA 98665
800.603.3005
www.wisewomanpress.com

Books by Emma Curtis Hopkins

- *Resume*
- *The Gospel Series*
- *Class Lessons of 1888*
- *Self Treatments including Radiant I Am*
- *High Mysticism*
- *Genesis Series 1894*
- *Esoteric Philosophy in Spiritual Science*
- *Drops of Gold Journal*
- *Judgment Series*
- *Bible Interpretations: Series I, thru XXII*

Books by Ruth L. Miller

- *Unveiling Your Hidden Power: Emma Curtis Hopkins' Metaphysics for the 21st Century*
- *Coming into Freedom: Emily Cady's Lessons in Truth for the 21st Century*
- *150 Years of Healing: The Founders and Science of New Thought*
- *Power Beyond Magic: Ernest Holmes Biography*
- *Power to Heal: Emma Curtis Hopkins Biography*
- *The Power of Unity: Charles Fillmore Biography*
- *Power of Thought: Phineas P. Quimby Biography*
- *The Power of Insight: Thomas Troward Biography*
- *The Power of the Self: Ralph Waldo Emerson Biography*
- *Uncommon Prayer*
- *Spiritual Success*
- *Finding the Path*

Books by Ute Maria Cedilla

- *The Mysticism of Emma Curtis Hopkins*
- *Volume 1 Finding the Christ*
- *Volume 2 Ministry: Realizing The Christ One in All*

List of Bible Interpretation Series with dates from 1st to 22nd Series.

This list is for the 1st to the 22nd Series. Emma produced twenty eight Series of Bible Interpretations.

She followed the Bible Passages provided by the International Committee of Clerics who produced the Bible Quotations for each year's use in churches all over the world.

Emma used these for her column of Bible Interpretations in both the Christian Science Magazine, at her Seminary and in the Chicago Inter-Ocean Newspaper.

First Series

July 5 - September 27, 1891

Lesson 1	The Word Made Flesh *John 1:1-18*	July 5th
Lesson 2	Christ's First Disciples John 1:29-42	July 12th
Lesson 3	All Is Divine Order *John 2:1-1*1 (Christ's first Miracle)	July 19th
Lesson 4	Jesus Christ and Nicodemus *John 3:1-17*	July 26th
Lesson 5	Christ at Samaria *John 4:5-26* (Christ at Jacob's Well)	August 2nd
Lesson 6	Self-condemnation *John 5:17-30* (Christ's Authority)	August 9th
Lesson 7	Feeding the Starving *John 6:1-14* (The Five Thousand Fed)	August 16th
Lesson 8	The Bread of Life *John 6:26-40* (Christ the Bread of Life)	August 23rd
Lesson 9	The Chief Thought *John 7:31-34* (Christ at the Feast)	August 30th
Lesson 10	Continue the Work *John 8:31-47*	September 6th
Lesson 11	Inheritance of Sin *John 9:1-11, 35-38* (Christ and the Blind Man)	September 13th
Lesson 12	The Real Kingdom *John 10:1-16* (Christ the Good Shepherd)	September 20th
Lesson 13	In Retrospection Review	September 27th

Second Series

October 4 - December 27, 1891

Lesson 1	Mary and Martha *John 11:21-44*	October 4th
Lesson 2	Glory of Christ *John 12:20-36*	October 11th
Lesson 3	Good in Sacrifice *John 13:1-17*	October 18th
Lesson 4	Power of the Mind *John 14:13; 15-27*	October 25th
Lesson 5	Vines and Branches *John 15:1-16*	November 1st
Lesson 6	Your Idea of God *John 16:1-15*	November 8th
Lesson 7	Magic of His Name *John 17:1-19*	November 15th
Lesson 8	Jesus and Judas *John 18:1-13*	November 22nd
Lesson 9	Scourge of Tongues *John 19:1-16*	November 29th
Lesson 10	Simplicity of Faith *John 19:17-30*	December 6th
Lesson 11	Christ is All in All *John 20: 1-18*	December 13th
Lesson 12	Risen With Christ *John 21:1-14*	December 20th
Lesson 13	The Spirit is Able Review of Year	December 27th

Third Series

January 3 - March 27, 1892

Lesson 1	A Golden Promise *Isaiah 11:1-10*	January 3rd
Lesson 2	The Twelve Gates *Isaiah 26:1-10*	January 10th
Lesson 3	Who Are Drunkards *Isaiah 28:1-13*	January 17th
Lesson 4	Awake Thou That Sleepest *Isaiah 37:1-21*	January 24th
Lesson 5	The Healing Light *Isaiah 53:1-21*	January 31st
Lesson 6	True Ideal of God *Isaiah 55:1-13*	February 7th
Lesson 7	Heaven Around Us *Jeremiah 31 14-37*	February 14th
Lesson 8	But One Substance *Jeremiah 36:19-31*	February 21st
Lesson 9	Justice of Jehovah *Jeremiah 37:11-21*	February 28th
Lesson 10	God and Man Are One *Jeremiah 39:1-10*	March 6th
Lesson 11	Spiritual Ideas *Ezekiel 4:9, 36:25-38*	March 13th
Lesson 12	All Flesh is Grass *Isaiah 40:1-10*	March 20th
Lesson 13	The Old and New Contrasted Review	March 27th

Fourth Series

April 3 - June 26, 1892

Lesson 1	Realm of Thought *Psalm 1:1-6*	April 3rd
Lesson 2	The Power of Faith *Psalm 2:1-12*	April 10th
Lesson 3	Let the Spirit Work *Psalm 19:1-14*	April 17th
Lesson 4	Christ is Dominion *Psalm 23:1-6*	April 24th
Lesson 5	External or Mystic *Psalm 51:1-13*	May 1st
Lesson 6	Value of Early Beliefs *Psalm 72: 1-9*	May 8th
Lesson 7	Truth Makes Free *Psalm 84:1-12*	May 15th
Lesson 8	False Ideas of God *Psalm 103:1-22*	May 22nd
Lesson 9	But Men Must Work *Daniel 1:8-21*	May 29th
Lesson 10	Artificial Helps *Daniel 2:36-49*	June 5th
Lesson 11	Dwelling in Perfect Life *Daniel 3:13-25*	June 12th
Lesson 12	Which Streak Shall Rule *Daniel 6:16-28*	June 19th
Lesson 13	See Things as They Are Review of 12 Lessons	June 26th

Fifth Series

July 3 - September 18, 1892

Lesson 1	The Measure of a Master *Acts 1:1-12*	July 3rd
Lesson 2	Chief Ideas Rule People *Acts 2:1-12*	July 10th
Lesson 3	New Ideas About Healing *Acts 2:37-47*	July 17th
Lesson 4	Heaven a State of Mind *Acts 3:1-16*	July 24th
Lesson 5	About Mesmeric Powers *Acts 4:1-18*	July 31st
Lesson 6	Points in the Mosaic Law *Acts 4:19-31*	August 7th
Lesson 7	Napoleon's Ambition *Acts 5:1-11*	August 14th
Lesson 8	A River Within the Heart *Acts 5:25-41*	August 21st
Lesson 9	The Answering of Prayer Acts 7: 54-60 - Acts 8: 1-4	August 28th
Lesson 10	Words Spoken by the Mind *Acts 8:5-35*	September 4th
Lesson 11	Just What It Teaches Us *Acts 8:26-40*	September 11th
Lesson 12	The Healing Principle Review	September 18th

Sixth Series

September 25 - December 18, 1892

Lesson 1	The Science of Christ 1 Corinthians 11:23-34	September 25th
Lesson 2	On the Healing of Saul Acts 9:1-31	October 2nd
Lesson 3	The Power of the Mind Explained Acts 9:32-43	October 9th
Lesson 4	Faith in Good to Come Acts 10:1-20	October 16th
Lesson 5	Emerson's Great Task Acts 10:30-48	October 23rd
Lesson 6	The Teaching of Freedom Acts 11:19-30	October 30th
Lesson 7	Seek and Ye Shall Find Acts 12:1-17	November 6th
Lesson 8	The Ministry of the Holy Mother Acts 13:1-13	November 13th
Lesson 9	The Power of Lofty Ideas Acts 13:26-43	November 20th
Lesson 10	Sure Recipe for Old Age Acts 13:44-52, 14:1-7	November 27th
Lesson 11	The Healing Principle Acts 14:8-22	December 4th
Lesson 12	Washington's Vision Acts 15:12-29	December 11th
Lesson 13	Review of the Quarter	December 18th
	Partial Lesson Shepherds and the Star	December 25th

Seventh Series

January 1 - March 31, 1893

Lesson 1	All is as Allah Wills *Ezra 1*	January 1st
Lesson 2	Zerubbabel's High Ideal *Ezra 2:8-13*	January 8th
Lesson 3	Divine Rays Of Power *Ezra 4*	January 15th
Lesson 4	Visions Of Zechariah *Zechariah 3*	January 22nd
Lesson 5	Spirit of the Land Zechariah 4:1-10	January 27th
Lesson 6	Dedicating the Temple Ezra 6:14-22	February 3rd
Lesson 7	Nehemiah's Prayer *Nehemiah 13*	February 12th
Lesson 8	Ancient Religions *Nehemiah 4*	February 19th
Lesson 9	Understanding is Strength Part 1 *Nehemiah 13*	February 26th
Lesson 10	Understanding is Strength Part 2 *Nehemiah 13*	March 3rd
Lesson 11	Way of the Spirit *Esther*	March 10th
Lesson 12	Speaking of Right Things Proverbs 23:15-23	March 17th
Lesson 13	Review	March 24th

Eighth Series

April 2 - June 25, 1893

Lesson 1	The Resurrection of Christ *Matthew 28:1-10*	April 2nd
Lesson 2	Universal Energy *Book of Job, Part 1*	April 9th
Lesson 3	Strength From Confidence *Book of Job, Part II*	April 16th
Lesson 4	The New Doctrine Brought Out *Book of Job, Part III*	April 23rd
Lesson 5	Wisdom's Warning *Proverbs 1:20-23*	April 30th
Lesson 6	The Law of Understanding *Proverbs 3*	May 7th
Lesson 7	Self-Esteem *Proverbs 12:1-15*	May 14th
Lesson 8	Physical vs. Spiritual Power *Proverbs 23:29-35*	May 21st
Lesson 9	Only One Power (information taken from Review)	May 28th
Lesson 10	Recognizing Our Spiritual Nature *Proverbs 31:10-31*	June 4th
Lesson 11	Intuition *Ezekiel 8:2-3, Ezekiel 9:3-6, 11*	June 11th
Lesson 12	The Power of Faith *Malachi*	June 18th
Lesson 13	Review of the 2nd Quarter *Proverbs 31:10-31*	June 25th

Ninth Series

July 2 - September 27, 1893

Lesson 1	Secret of all Power *Acts 16: 6-15*	July 2nd
Lesson 2	The Flame of Spiritual Verity *Acts 16:18*	July 9th
Lesson 3	Healing Energy Gifts *Acts 18:19-21*	July 16th
Lesson 4	Be Still My Soul *Acts 17:16-24*	July 23rd
Lesson 5	(Missing) Acts 18:1-11	July 30th
Lesson 6	Missing No Lesson *	August 6th
Lesson 7	The Comforter is the Holy Ghost *Acts 20*	August 13th
Lesson 8	Conscious of a Lofty Purpose *Acts 21*	August 20th
Lesson 9	Measure of Understanding *Acts 24:19-32*	August 27th
Lesson 10	The Angels of Paul *Acts 23:25-26*	September 3rd
Lesson 11	The Hope of Israel *Acts 28:20-31*	September 10th
Lesson 12	Joy in the Holy Ghost *Romans 14*	September 17th
Lesson 13	Review *Acts 26-19-32*	September 24th

Tenth Series

October 1 – December 24, 1893

Lesson 1	When the Truth is Known *Romans 1:1-19*	October 1st
Lesson 2	Justification, free grace, redemption *Romans 3:19-26*	October 8th.
Lesson 3	Justification by Faith *Romans 5:1-11* *Romans 12:1-15*	October 15th
Lesson 4	Christian Living *Romans 12:1*	October 22nd
Lesson 5	Comments on the Golden Text *I Corinthians 8:1-13*	October 29th
Lesson 6	Science of the Christ Principle *I Corinthians 12:1-26*	November 5th
Lesson 7	The Grace of Liberality *II Corinthians 8:1-12*	November 12th
Lesson 8	Imitation of Christ *Ephesians 4:20-32*	November 19th
Lesson 9	The Christian Home *Colossians 3:12-25*	November 26th
Lesson 10	*Grateful Obedience* *James 1:16-27*	December 3rd
Lesson 11	The Heavenly Inheritance *I Peter 1:1-12*	December 10th
Lesson 12	The Glorified Saviour *Revelation 1:9-20*	December 17th
Lesson 13	A Christmas Lesson Matthew 2:1-11	December 24th
Lesson 14	Review	December 31st

Eleventh Series

January 1 – March 25, 1894

Lesson 1	The First Adam *Genesis 1:26-31 & 2:1-3*	January 7th
Lesson 2	Adam's Sin and God's Grace *Genesis 3:1-15*	January 14th
Lesson 3	Cain and Abel *Genesis 4:3-13*	January 21st
Lesson 4	God's Covenant With Noah *Genesis 9:8-17*	January 28th
Lesson 5	Beginning of the Hebrew Nation *Genesis 12:1-9*	February 4th
Lesson 6	God's Covenant With Abram *Genesis 17:1-9*	February 11th
Lesson 7	God's Judgment of Sodom *Genesis 18:22-23*	February 18th
Lesson 8	Trial of Abraham's Faith *Genesis 22:1-13*	February 25th
Lesson 9	Selling the Birthright *Genesis 25:27-34*	March 4th
Lesson 10	Jacob at Bethel *Genesis 28:10-22*	March 11th
Lesson 11	Temperance *Proverbs 20:1-7*	March 18th
Lesson 12	Review and Easter *Mark 16:1-8*	March 25th

Twelfth Series

April 1 – June 24, 1894

Lesson 1	Jacob's Prevailing Prayer *Genesis 24:30, 32:9-12*	April 8th
Lesson 2	Discord in Jacob's Family *Genesis 37:1-11*	April 1st
Lesson 3	Joseph Sold into Egypt *Genesis 37:23-36*	April 15th
Lesson 4	Object Lesson in Genesis *Genesis 41:38-48*	April 22nd
Lesson 5	"With Thee is Fullness of Joy" *Genesis 45:1-15*	April 29th
Lesson 6	Change of Heart *Genesis 50:14-26*	May 6th
Lesson 7	Israel in Egypt *Exodus 1:1-14*	May 13th
Lesson 8	The Childhood of Moses *Exodus 2:1-10*	May 20th
Lesson 9	Moses Sent As A Deliverer *Exodus 3:10-20*	May 27th
Lesson 10	The Passover Instituted *Exodus 12:1-14*	June 3rd
Lesson 11	Passage of the Red Sea *Exodus 14:19-29*	June 10th
Lesson 12	The Woes of the Drunkard *Proverbs 23:29-35*	June 17th
Lesson 13	Review	June 24th

Thirteenth Series

July 1 – September 30, 1894

Lesson 1	The Birth of Jesus *Luke 2:1-16*	July 1st
Lesson 2	Presentation in the Temple *Luke 2:25-38*	July 8th
Lesson 3	Visit of the Wise Men *Matthew 1:2-12*	July 15th
Lesson 4	Flight Into Egypt *Mathew 2:13-23*	July 22nd
Lesson 5	The Youth of Jesus *Luke2:40-52*	July 29th
Lesson 6	The "All is God" Doctrine *Luke 2:40-52*	August 5th
Lesson 7	Missing	August 12th
Lesson 8	First Disciples of Jesus *John 1:36-49*	August 19th
Lesson 9	The First Miracle of Jesus *John 2:1-11*	August 26th
Lesson 10	Jesus Cleansing the Temple *John 2:13-25*	September 2nd
Lesson 11	Jesus and Nicodemus *John 3:1-16*	September 9th
Lesson 12	Jesus at Jacob's Well *John 4:9-26*	September 16th
Lesson 13	Daniel's Abstinence *Daniel 1:8-20*	September 23rd
Lesson 14	Review *John 2:13-25*	September 30th

Fourteenth Series

October 7 – December 30, 1894

Lesson 1	Jesus At Nazareth *Luke 4:16-30*	October 7th
Lesson 2	The Draught of Fishes *Luke 5:1-11*	October 14th
Lesson 3	The Sabbath in Capernaum *Mark 1:21-34*	October 21st
Lesson 4	The Paralytic Healed *Mark 2:1-12*	October 28th
Lesson 5	Reading of Sacred Books *Mark 2:23-38, Mark 3:1-5*	November 4th
Lesson 6	Spiritual Executiveness *Mark 3:6-19*	November 11th
Lesson 7	Twelve Powers Of The Soul *Luke 6:20-31*	November 18th
Lesson 8	Things Not Understood Attributed to Satan *Mark 3:22-35*	November 25th
Lesson 9	Independence of Mind *Luke 7:24-35*	December 2nd
Lesson 10	The Gift of Untaught Wisdom *Luke 8:4-15*	December 9th
Lesson 11	The Divine Eye Within *Matthew 5:5-16*	December 16th
Lesson 12	Unto Us a Child I s Born *Luke 7:24-35*	December 23rd
Lesson 13	Review *Isaiah 9:2-7*	December 30th

Fifteenth Series

January 6-March 31, 1895

Lesson 1	Missing *Mark 6:17-29*	January 6th
Lesson 2	The Prince Of The World *Mark 6:30-44*	January 13th
Lesson 3	The Golden Text *John 6:25-35*	January 20th
Lesson 4	The Golden Text *Matthew 16:13-25*	January 27th
Lesson 5	The Transfiguration *Luke 9:28-36*	February 3rd
Lesson 6	Christ And The Children *Matthew 18:1-14*	February 10th
Lesson 7	The Good Samaritan *Luke 10:25-37*	February 17th
Lesson 8	Christ And The Man Born Blind *John 9:1-11*	February 24th
Lesson 9	The Raising Of Lazarus *John 11:30-45*	March 3rd
Lesson 10	The Rich Young Ruler *Mark 10:17-27*	March 10th
Lesson 11	Zaccheus The Publican *Luke 1:10*	March 17th
Lesson 12	Purity Of Life *Romans 13:8-14*	March 24th
Lesson 13	Review	March 31st

Sixteenth Series

April 7-June 30, 1895

Lesson 1	The Triumphal Entry *Mark 11:1-11*	April 7th
Lesson 2	The Easter Lesson *Mark 12:1-12*	April 14th
Lesson 3	Watchfulness Mark 24:42-51	April 21st
Lesson 4	The Lord's Supper *Mark 14:12-26*	April 28th
Lesson 5	Jesus in Gethsemane Mark 15:42-52	May 5th
Lesson 6	The Jesus Christ Power *Mark 14:53-72*	May 12th
Lesson 7	Jesus Before Pilate *Mark 15:1-15*	May 19th
Lesson 8	The Day of the Crucifixion *Mark 15:22-37*	May 26th
Lesson 9	At the Tomb *Mark 16:1-8*	June 2nd
Lesson 10	The Road To Emmaus *Luke 24:13-32*	June 9th
Lesson 11	Fisher of Men *John 21:4-17*	June 16th
Lesson 12	Missing Luke 24:27-29	June 23rd
Lesson 13	Review	June 30th

Seventeenth Series

July 7 – September 29, 1895

Lesson 1	The Bread of Energy *Exodus 22:1-17*	July 7th
Lesson 2	Grandeur is Messiahship *Exodus 32:30-35*	July 14th
Lesson 3	Temperance *Leviticus 10:1-9*	July 21st
Lesson 4	The Alluring Heart of Man *Numbers 10:29-36*	July 28th
Lesson 5	As a Man Thinketh Numbers 13:17-23	August 4th
Lesson 6	Rock of Eternal Security *Numbers 31:4-9*	August 11th
Lesson 7	Something Behind *Deuteronomy 6:3-15*	August 18th
Lesson 8	What You See Is What You Get *Joshua 3:5-17*	August 25th
Lesson 9	Every Man To His Miracle *Joshua 6:8-20*	September 1st
Lesson 10	Every Man To His Harvest *Joshua 14:5-14*	September 8th
Lesson 11	Every Man To His Refuge *Joshua 20:1-9*	September 15th
Lesson 12	The Twelve Propositions Joshua 24:14-25	September 22nd
Lesson 13	Review I Kings 8:56	September 29th

Eighteenth Series

Oct 6 – December 29, 1895

Lesson 1	Missing	October 6th
Lesson 2	Gideon's Triumph *Judges 7:13-23*	October 13th
Lesson 3	The Divine Ego *Ruth 1:4-22*	October 20th
Lesson 4	All is Good *I Samuel 3:1-11*	October 27th
Lesson 5	If Thine Eye Be Single *I Samuel 7:5-12*	November 3rd
Lesson 6	Saul Chosen King *I Samuel 10:17-27*	November 10th
Lesson 7	Saul Rejected *I Samuel 15:10-23*	November 17th
Lesson 8	Temperance *Isaiah 5:11*	November 24th
Lesson 9	The Lord Looketh Upon the Heart *I Samuel 16:1-13*	December 1st
Lesson 10	Missing	December 8th
Lesson 11	The Third Influence *I Samuel 20:32-42*	December 15th
Lesson 12	The Doctrine of the Holy Land *Luke 2:8-9*	December 22nd
Lesson 13	Review	December 29th

Nineteenth Series

January 5 – March 29, 1896

Lesson 1	Missing	January 5th
Lesson 2	Missing	January 12th
Lesson 3	Lesson on Repentance *Luke 3:15-22*	January 19th
Lesson 4	"The Early Ministry of Jesus" *Luke 4:22*	January 26th
Lesson 5	Missing	February 2nd
Lesson 6	Missing	February 9th
Lesson 7	The Secret Note *Luke 6:41-49*	February 16th
Lesson 8	Answered Prayer *Luke 6:41-49*	February 23rd
Lesson 9	Letting Go The Old Self *Luke 9:18-27*	March 1st
Lesson 10	"Me, Imperturbed" *Luke 10:25-37*	March 8th
Lesson 11	Lord's Prayer *Luke 11:1-13*	March 15th
Lesson 12	Be Not Drunk With Wine *Luke 12:37-46*	March 22nd
Lesson 13	The Winds of Living Light *Luke 12:8*	March 29th

Emma Curtis Hopkins was absent on a voyage to Vera Cruz, Mexico to bring her ill son back to the USA. She left December 28, 1895 and returned February 6, 1896. This would account for missing lessons in this quarter. She may have mailed the two in January or they may have been written previously.

Twentieth Series

April 5 – June 28, 1896

Lesson 1	The Radiation of Light *Luke 13:22-30*	April 5
Lesson 2	The Great Supper *Luke 14:15-24*	April 12th
Lesson 3	The Radiation of Joy *Luke 15:11-24*	April 19th
Lesson 4	Out of the Range of Mind *Luke 16:19-31*	April 26th
Lesson 5	Going Toward Jerusalem *Luke 17:5-10*	May 3rd
Lesson 6	The Publican And The Pharisee *Luke 18:9-17*	May 10th
Lesson 7	The Last Great Week *Luke 19:11-27*	May 17th
Lesson 8	Unthinkable Divinity *Luke 20:9-19*	May 24th
Lesson 9	The Destruction Of Jerusalem Foretold *Luke 21:20-36*	May 31st
Lesson 10	Forgiveness for Hunger *Luke 22:22-47*	June 7th
Lesson 11	Forgiveness for the Unknown and the Undone *Luke 23:33-46*	June 14th
Lesson 12	The Risen Lord *Luke 24:36-53*	June 21st
Lesson 13	Review	June 28th

Twenty-First Series

July 5 – September 27, 1896

Lesson 1	The Lord Reigneth	July 5th
	II Samuel 2:1-11	
Lesson 2	Adeptship	July 12th
	II Samuel 5:1-12	
Lesson 3	The Ark	July 19th
	II Samuel 6:1-12	
Lesson 4	Purpose of An Adept	July 26th
	II Samuel 7:4-16	
Lesson 5	Individual Emancipatioin	August 2nd
	II Samuel 9:1-13	
Lesson 6	The Almighty Friend	August 9th
	II Samuel 10:8-19	
Lesson 7	Salvation Is Emancipation(missing)	August 16th
	Psalms 32:1-1	
Lesson 8	Individual Emancipation	August 23rd
	II Samuel 15:1-12	
Lesson 9	Absalom's Defeat And Death	August 30th
	II Samuel 16:9-17	
Lesson 10	The Crown Of Effort	September 6th
	I Chronicles 22:6-16	
Lesson 11	"Thy Gentleness Hath Made Me Great	
	II Samuel 22	September 13th
Lesson 12	A Fool For Christ's Sake	September 20th
	Proverbs 16:7-33	
Lesson 13	The Lord is a Strong Tower	September 27th
	Proverbs 28:10	

September 27 of this quarter is a Review of the International Committee listing, not Emma's usual listing and review of the previous lessons in the quarter.

Twenty-Second Series

October 4 – December 27, 1896

Lesson 1	A Study in the Science of the Lightning	
	I Kings 1	October 4th
Lesson 2	Solomon's Wise Choice	October 11th
	I Kings 3	
Lesson 3	The Mysterious Adeptship Inherent In Us All	
	I Kings 4:25-34	October 18th
Lesson 4	Missing	October 25th
Lesson 5	Building the Temple	November 1st
	I Kings 5:1-12	
Lesson 6	The Dedication of the Temple	November 8th
	I Kings 8:54-63	
Lesson 7	Converse With the Actual God	November 15th
	I Kings 9:1-9	
Lesson 8	Rewards of Obedience	November 22nd
	Proverbs 3:1-17	
Lesson 9	A Greater Than Solomon	November 29th
	I Kings 10:1	
Lesson 10	Our Destined End or Way	December 6th
	I Kings 11:4-13, II Corinthians 10:12	
Lesson 11	Solomon's Son	December 13th
	Proverbs 23:15-25	
Lesson 12	Missing	December 20th
Lesson 13	Review	December 27th
	Ecclesiastes 12:13	

www.ingramcontent.com/pod-product-compliance
Lightning Source LLC
Chambersburg PA
CBHW062223080426
42734CB00010B/2000